The
SCARLET THREAD
OF THE BIBLE

Behold the Lamb

WALT THRUN

WESTBOW
PRESS®
A DIVISION OF THOMAS NELSON
& ZONDERVAN

WestBow Press books may be ordered through booksellers or by contacting:

WestBow Press
A Division of Thomas Nelson & Zondervan
1663 Liberty Drive
Bloomington, IN 47403
www.westbowpress.com
844-714-3454

Because of the dynamic nature of the Internet, any web addresses or links contained in this book may have changed since publication and may no longer be valid. The views expressed in this work are solely those of the author and do not necessarily reflect the views of the publisher, and the publisher hereby disclaims any responsibility for them.

Any people depicted in stock imagery provided by Getty Images are models, and such images are being used for illustrative purposes only.
Certain stock imagery © Getty Images.

Scripture taken from the NEW AMERICAN STANDARD BIBLE®, Copyright © 1960,1962,1963,1968,1971,1972,1973,1975,1977,1995 by The Lockman Foundation. Used by permission. www.Lockman.org

Scripture taken from the New King James Version® Copyright © 1982 by Thomas Nelson. Used by permission. All rights reserved.

ISBN: 978-1-6642-0248-1 (sc)
ISBN: 978-1-6642-0249-8 (e)

Print information available on the last page.

WestBow Press rev. date: 10/06/2020

Dedication

This book is dedicated to my bride of 55 years who beat me home to the next stage of our eternal journey.

I met Patt in 1960 while I was serving in the Marine Corp in Southern California. She was very active in an American Baptist Church in Anaheim, having served on the youth council at the state level during her late teen years.

We married in that church the following year on March 17th, which was also the twenty fifth anniversary of her parents.

One of the guests at our wedding told me that I better take good care of her inasmuch as she was a very special girl. That guest's name was Dewey Lockman, the president of the Lockman Foundation, who produced the New American Standard Bible.

The first copyright of that Bible was in 1960. They published the New Testament in 1963 and the Old Testament in 1971.

Needless to say, Patt's Bible was a NASB translation. During the following decades she made countless notes and underlines in her sacred book.

I cherish her Bible, and in fact used that Bible with all the markings as the predominant translation for this book.

The **Scarlet Thread of the Bible** contains more than 500 verses quoted from her NASB.

It was a wonderful experience; in fact, it was like we were doing a Bible study together again, and isn't 'together' a beautiful word.

Introduction

The purpose and role of blood in the human body is extremely significant.

Blood supplies oxygen and nutrients to tissues, removes waste, transports hormones and other signals throughout the body, and regulates body pH and core body temperatures.

Subsequently, blood regulates the body's systems and maintains homeostasis which is defined as the ability to maintain internal stability in an organism to compensate for environmental changes, such as maintaining body temperature at 98.6 degrees.

Blood, therefore, is the sustainer of life.

As might be expected then, when a first responder arrives on the scene of an injury accident, an initial action, and major aim, is to stop the loss of blood of the injured.

The significance of blood was recorded in the Bible some 3,400 years ago. The word occurs nearly 500 times in the Bible.

One of the foundational passages in the entire Bible is:

"For the life of the flesh is in the blood..."
Leviticus 17:11a NKJV

The Hebrew word for 'life' in this verse is *Nephesh* defined as the soul by which the body lives by drawing breath. Soul is the inner part of man.

Likewise, the Hebrew for 'flesh' is *Basar* defined as a created living creature. It defines the external form of a person. Flesh is weak, temporary, corruptible (subject to decay), and mortal.

The predominant Hebrew word for 'blood' is *Dam* defined as the very essence of life as defined above. Thus, the shedding of blood results in loss of life, or death.

Then God told Moses to tell the people the significance of the blood and its predominant purpose in the Bible.

"...and I have given it to you upon the altar to make atonement for your souls; for it is the blood that makes atonement for the soul."
Leviticus 17:11b NKJV

The Hebrew word for atonement in this verse is *Kapar* defined as 'reconcile' or 'appease.'

Other similar, and related, Hebrew words are *Kaphos* meaning 'cover,' and *Kopher* meaning 'ransom' or 'satisfaction.'

God revealed the sanctity of blood in the first book of the Bible.

"Whoever sheds man's blood, by man his blood shall be shed for in the image of God He made man."
Genesis 9:6 NKJV

That verse introduced capital punishment for the shedding of blood, and it has never been rescinded.

Another very significant Hebrew word for blood is *Netsach* with the primary meaning the 'brilliant juice of grapes.'

Jacob used *Netsach* when prophesying about his son Judah's future.

"Binding his donkey to the vine, and his donkey's colt to the choice vine, he washed his garments in wine, and his clothes in the blood (Netsach) of grapes."
Genesis 49:11 NKJV

The application of this verse will be covered in detail in this book.

Thus, the blood of animals was sacrificed to God as a substitute to 'cover' the sins of the one who sinned in the Old Testament.

Mankind had a problem; however…

"For it is not possible that the blood of bulls and goats could take away sins."
Hebrews 10:4 NKJV

Contents

Dedication v

Introduction.. vii

Chapter 1   Blood in Offerings... 1

Chapter 2   Blood in Israel's Sacred Feast Days 37

Chapter 3   Blood in Ratifying Covenants.................... 88

Chapter 4   The New Covenant also Ratified with
             Blood... 103

Chapter 5   Water Turns to Blood, and Blood is
             One with Wine 153

Chapter 6   The Shedding of Innocent Blood
             Requires Death.. 166

Chapter 7   The Ultimate Bloodshed – Behold the
             Lamb 182

Chapter 1

Blood in Offerings

Offerings can be traced back to the sons of Adam and Eve. Chapter 1 will describe the varied offerings prescribed primarily to Moses shortly after the Exodus from Egypt.

One of the primary premises of this chapter, and in fact the entire book, is the required shedding of blood, resulting in death, required for atonement for sin. The shed blood of the offering is a substitute for the shed blood of the offender.

The first example of shed blood of an animal to atone for sin was when God covered Adam and Eve with the skins of animals to replace leaves as their covering when God sent them out of the Garden.

Sub headings in Chapter 1 include:

- **Burnt Offerings (daily, Sabbaths, monthly)**
- **Burnt Offerings before Moses, Time of Abraham, and Time of the Kings**
- **Grain Offerings**
- **Salt in Grain Offerings**
- **Salt in the New Testament**
- **Peace Offerings**
- **Sin Offerings for Anointed Priest, Ruler or Leader, Individual, or Whole congregation**
- **Trespass (Guilt) Offerings**
- **Trespass Offerings with Restitution**

- **Heave Offerings**
- **Wave Offerings**
- **Dealing with Intentional Sins**
- **Offerings of the Future**

Chapter 2

Blood in Israel's Sacred Feast Days

Chapter 2 begins with a Hebrew Calendar showing the seven Feasts, or Sacred Days, for Israel and the month and day, or days, of their observance.

Each Feast or Sacred Day will be described along with what each Feast and Sacred Day signifies.

Also the Feasts that have been fulfilled will be identified.

Sub headings in Chapter 2 include:

- **Passover**
- **The Fulfillment of Passover**
- **Feast of Unleavened Bread**
- **Feast of First Fruits**
- **Feast of Weeks**
- **From the Feast of Weeks to Pentecost**
- **Feast of Trumpets**
- **Day of Atonement**
- **Feast of Tabernacles**
- **Daily Offerings to be Reinstated preceding the Tribulation**
- **Traditional Feasts and Offerings in the Millennial Kingdom**
- **Other Offerings in the Millennial Kingdom**

Chapter 3

Blood in Ratifying Covenants

Chapter 3 begins with detailed instructions by God to Abram to leave his homeland to go to a new place where pagan gods were not worshipped.

Abram obeyed and God subsequently confirmed His instructions and promise with an everlasting covenant which He ratified unilaterally.

This chapter will also include the preparation of the tabernacle and priesthood to administer God's plan for His people.

Sub headings in chapter 3 include:

- **The Abrahamic Covenant and its Unilateral Ratification**
- **Subsequent Biblical References to the Abrahamic Covenant**
- **Another Significant Covenant Ratified with Blood (the Old Covenant)**
- **Plans for the Earthly Tabernacle to be Patterned after the Heavenly**
- **Aaron and his Sons Consecrated with Blood in Preparation to Serve in the Tabernacle shortly after the Law was Given**
- **Israel Broke the Old Covenant**

Chapter 4

The New Covenant also Ratified with Blood

The New Covenant was inevitable inasmuch as the Israelites broke the old. In fact it was impossible to fulfill the old. Of course, God knew that from the beginning.

The shortfalls of the old will be discussed and details of the new will be presented.

The majority of chapter 3 will in essence be an expository on the Book of Hebrews which discusses the requirements of the New Covenant, the requirements of the mediator of such a covenant, and the requirements of the High Priest to enact the covenant.

Sub headings in chapter 4 include:

- **Jesus fulfilled the 'Old'**
- **The New Covenant Described**
- **The prophets spoke of the Spirit to come to Israel in the Future**
- **The Holy Spirit; however, is the Heart of the Church Today**
- **National Israel Waits for what the Church already Has**
- **Christ is the Mediator of the New Covenant**
- **The Testator must first Die before His Will and Testament is Enacted**
- **Christ is also the Ultimate High Priest**

- As the Son of God, Jesus the High Priest is Superior to Angels
- Comparing Moses with the Ultimate High Priest
- The Work of the High Priest brings Rest
- Melchizedek and the Ultimate High Priest
- Jesus' Qualification for High Priest
- The Levitical Priesthood was only a Foreshadow for Better Things
- As the Original Tabernacle was Patterned after the Heavenly, so was the Priesthood which Served in the Earthly Tabernacle
- High Priestly Duties, the Old vs. the New
- The Unforgivable Sin

Chapter 5

Water Turns to Blood, and Blood is One with Wine

Blood, water, and wine are intrinsically mixed throughout the Bible.

This chapter will begin with water turning to blood as the first of ten plagues on Egypt preceding the Exodus, and end in the final chapters of the Book of Revelation.

Sub headings of Chapter 5 include:

- **Water Turns to Blood (in Egypt and in the latter days)**
- **Blood at the Height of God's Wrath**
- **Blood is the Required Payment for Sin**
- **Blood and Wine**

Chapter 6

The Shedding of Innocent Blood Requires Death

Inasmuch as blood is the life of the flesh, and God created man in His own image, the shedding of innocent blood requires death of the one who sheds the blood.

This chapter will reveal that one of the most abominable of Israel's sins was the shedding of innocent blood, along with harlotry and idolatry.

Sub headings of chapter 6 include:

- **The Killing of Infants**
- **The Shedding of Blood of the Innocent was/is always Condemned**
- **Bloodshed by Malice**
- **Israel's Sin of Blood Shedding and the Consequences**
- **Duties of the Watchman**
- **Examples of Bloodshed in the New Testament**

Chapter 7

The Ultimate Bloodshed – Behold the Lamb

Chapter 7 will bring the book to its conclusion.

The entire Bible centers on the concept of shed blood and substitution.

While many individuals, and churches, avoid proclaiming the significance of the blood, the true believer will embrace that teaching. Christians realize that if it wasn't for the substitutionary, vicarious, voluntary shedding of the blood of Christ to redeem sinners, each sinner would deserve to be on that cross paying for their own sins.

Recall, 'for all have sinned…'

Sub headings of chapter 7 include:

- **The significance of substitution (Abraham and Isaac)**
- **Other events where a lamb was the sacrifice, or substitute**
- **The ultimate Passover Lamb**
- **Jesus was about to die**
- **The trial of Jesus**
- **Apostolic teaching on the shed blood of Christ**
- **From the Book of Revelation**

Chapter 1

Blood in Offerings

The typical Hebrew word for offerings is *Qorban* which means a sacrificial present, an oblation, or a gift in the form of a sacrifice.

That quickly reminds us of the Pharisees who denied providing care for their parents using Corban as their excuse.

...but you say, "If a man says to his father or his mother, anything of mine you might have been helped by is Corban (that is to say, given to God)."
Mark 7:11 NASB

There are five basic offerings detailed in the Pentateuch.

- Burnt Offerings
- Grain Offerings
- Peace Offerings
- Sin Offerings
- Trespass Offerings

Burnt Offerings

The burnt offering is the most widely used. A major application of the burnt offering is made by, and for, an individual to recognize his general sinfulness, not for a specific transgression. The offering was a voluntary offering of repentance.

God spoke to Moses and outlined the requirements for burnt offerings for an individual.

"Speak to the sons of Israel and say to them, 'When any man of you brings an offering to the LORD, you shall bring your offering of animals from the herd or the flock.

If his offering is a burnt offering from the herd, he shall offer it a male without defect; he shall offer it at the doorway of the tent of meeting, that he may be accepted before the LORD.

And he shall lay his hand of the head of the burnt offering, that it may be accepted for him to make atonement on his behalf.

And he shall slay the young bull before the LORD; and Aaron's sons, the priests, shall offer up the blood and sprinkle the blood around on the altar that is at the doorway of the tent of meeting.

He shall then skin the burnt offering and cut it into its pieces.'"
Leviticus 1:2-6 NASB

If the one making the offering couldn't afford a bull, he could offer a male of the flock (sheep or goat), turtle doves, or young pigeons.

Several summary points of the burnt offering include:

- The offering must be voluntary
- The offering was a substitute for the one making the offering to make atonement for his general sinful nature
- The offering could be a bull, sheep or goat from the flock, a male without blemish
- The one making the offering must put his hand on the head of the animal and kill it
- The priests would sprinkle the blood around the altar
- The priests would skin the animal and then cut it into its prescribed pieces
- The priests would wash the entrails and legs with water
- The sacrifice, whether an animal or bird, would be completely burnt up producing a sweet, pleasing aroma to the LORD
- The skin of the animal offered was the only part that the priest could keep

Burnt offerings were offered on the 'altar of burnt sacrifice' which was located closest to the door of the tabernacle. The fire on that altar was to burn perpetually; it was never to go out.

Burnt offerings were also made for the whole congregation at prescribed times including daily, on the Sabbath day, and monthly.

Daily Burnt Offerings

Then God explained the requirements for the daily burnt offering.

"Now this is what you shall offer on the altar; two one year old lambs each day, continuously.

The one lamb you shall offer in the morning, and the other lamb you shall offer at twilight (between the two evenings);

...and there shall be one-tenth of an ephah of fine flour mixed with one-fourth of a hin of beaten oil, and one-fourth of a hin of wine for a libation (drink offering) for one lamb.

And the other lamb you shall offer at twilight (between the two evenings), and shall offer as the grain offering of the morning, with its libation (drink offering), for a soothing aroma, an offering by fire to the LORD.

It shall be a continual burnt offering throughout your generations at the doorway of the tent of meeting before the LORD, where I will speak to you there."
Exodus 29:38-42 NASB

As with the burnt offering made by the individual, all of the lambs offered would be completely burnt. Only the skins would remain and given to the priests.

"Also the priest who presents any man's burnt offering, that priest shall have for himself the skin of the burnt offering which he has presented."
Leviticus 7:8 NASB

Also, burnt offerings for the whole congregation would include a grain offering as well as a drink offering. An *ephah* is equivalent to about two-thirds of a bushel, while a *hin* equates to approximately 1.5 gallons.

The lamb offered at twilight would include the same grain and drink offering as with the lamb offered in the morning.

Burnt Offerings on the Sabbath

"Then on the Sabbath day two male lambs one year old without defect, and two-tenths of a measure of fine flour mixed with oil as a grain offering, and its libation (drink offering).

The burnt offering of every Sabbath is in addition to the continual burnt offering and its libation."
Numbers 28:9-10 NASB

Note that this burnt offering on the Sabbath was in addition to the regular daily burnt offerings. Even though both included two lambs of the first year, the grain offered for each lamb was different than with the daily burnt offerings.

Monthly Burnt Offerings

"Then at the beginning of each of your months you shall present a burnt offering to the LORD; two bulls and one ram, seven male lambs one year old without defect,

...and three-tenths of a measure of fine flour for a grain offering, mixed with oil, for each bull; and two-tenths of fine flour for a grain offering, mixed with oil, for the one ram;

...and a tenth of a measure of fine flour mixed with oil for a grain offering for each lamb, for a burnt offering of a soothing aroma, an offering by fire to the LORD.

And their libations (drink offering) shall be half a hin of wine for a bull and a third of a hin for the ram and a fourth of a hin for a lamb; this is the burnt offering of each month throughout the months of the year.

And one male goat for a sin offering to the LORD; it shall be offered with its libation (drink offering) in addition to the continual burnt offering."
Numbers 28:11-16 NASB

A more common name for monthly burnt offerings was New Moon offering. This was defined when the first glimpse of the new moon was visible which began a new month.

The New Moon offering was more detailed than the other burnt offerings. More animals were offered and the accompanying grain and drink offerings were different for each animal than in the other burnt offerings.

And while the New Moon offering was first mentioned during the forty years in the wilderness, the offering is thereafter mentioned throughout the Old Testament.

Burnt Offerings before the Time of Moses

The first indication of an offering in the Bible is found in the early chapters of Genesis.

After the sin of the first couple in the Garden of Eden, they were banished from the garden on the east side.

But just before they left, God did a very significant thing.

And the LORD God made garments of skin for Adam and his wife, and clothed them.
Genesis 3:21 NASB

Although there is no reference to a burnt offering, some animal had to shed its blood in order for God to clothe Adam and Eve with garments of skin.

And then we learn of two sons born to Adam and Eve, i.e. Cain and Abel. Each made an offering to God.

So it came about in the course of time that Cain brought an offering to the LORD of the fruit of the ground.

And Abel, on his part also brought of the firstlings of his flock and of their fat portions. And the LORD had regard for Abel and for his offering;

...but for Cain and for his offering He had no regard. So Cain became very angry and his countenance fell.
Genesis 4:3-5 NASB

Then centuries later, after the flood receded, Noah made an offering to God.

Then Noah built an altar to the LORD, and took of every clean animal and of every clean bird and offered burnt offerings on the altar.

And the LORD smelled the soothing aroma; and the LORD said to Himself, "I will never again curse the ground on account of man, for the intent of man's heart is evil from his youth; and I will never again destroy every living thing, as I have done."
Genesis 8:20-21 NASB

Burnt Offerings in the Time of Abraham

Now it came about after these things, that God tested Abraham, and said to him, "Abraham!" And he said, "Here I am."

And He said, "Take now your son, your only son, whom you love, Isaac, and go to the land of Moriah; and offer him

*there as a burnt offering on one of the mountains of which
I will tell you."*
Genesis 22:1-2 NASB

Abraham was obedient to the detail and was totally
willing to offer up his son Isaac as a burnt offering.

God was pleased with Abraham's obedience and
presented a substitute for the burnt offering instead of
Abraham's son.

*Then Abraham raised his eyes and looked, and behold,
behind him a ram caught in the thicket by his horns; and
Abraham went and took the ram, and offered him up for a
burnt offering in the place of his son.*
Genesis 22:13 NASB

Burnt Offerings during the Time of the Kings

King Solomon began to rule in 971 BC. Eleven years
later he dedicated the temple he had built for the LORD.

*Now when Solomon had finished praying, fire came
down from heaven and consumed the burnt offering and
the sacrifices; and the glory of the LORD filled the house
(temple).*
2 Chronicles 7:1 NASB

The actual dedication followed Solomon's prayer.

*Now the king and all Israel with him offered sacrifice
before the LORD.*

And Solomon offered for the sacrifice of peace offerings, which he offered to the LORD, 22,000 oxen and 120,000 sheep. So the king and all the sons of Israel dedicated the house of the LORD.
1 Kings 8:62-63 NASB

Needless to say the altar of burnt offering could not handle the size of the offering.

On the same day the king consecrated the middle of the court that was before the house of the LORD, because there he offered the burnt offering and the grain offering and the fat of the peace offerings;

...for the bronze altar that was before the LORD was too small to hold the burnt offering and the grain offering and the fat of the peace offerings.
1 Kings 8:64 NASB

Shortly thereafter, Solomon made regular sacrifices and offerings.

Then Solomon offered burnt offerings to the LORD on the altar of the LORD which he had built before the porch;

...and did so according to the daily rule, offering them up according to the commandment of Moses, for the Sabbaths, the new moons, and the three annual feasts – the Feast of Unleavened Bread, the Feast of Weeks, and the Feast of Booths (Tabernacles).
2 Chronicles 8:12-13 NASB

And then approximately two hundred years after Solomon, King Hezekiah of Judah reigned. He also followed Solomon's example and reinstated sacrifices and offerings.

And Hezekiah appointed the divisions of the priests and the Levites...for burnt offerings and for peace offerings, to minister and to give thanks and to praise in the gates of the camp of the LORD.

He also appointed the king's portion of his goods for the burnt offerings, namely, for the morning and evening burnt offerings,

...and the burnt offerings for the Sabbaths and for the new moons and for the fixed festivals, as it is written in the law of the LORD.
2 Chronicles 31:2-3 NASB

Grain Offerings

The Grain Offering represented the fruit of the land and did not include the sacrifice of living animals or birds. Grain offerings were, however, offered with burnt offerings and peace offerings as explained previously.

"Now when anyone presents a grain offering as an offering to the LORD, his offering shall be of fine flour, and he shall pour oil on it and put frankincense on it.

He shall then bring it to Aaron's sons, the priests; and shall take from it his handful of its fine flour and of its oil with all of its frankincense. And the priest shall offer it up in smoke as its memorial (reminder) portion on the altar, an offering by fire of a soothing aroma to the LORD.

And the remainder of the grain offering belongs to Aaron and his sons: a thing most holy, of the offerings to the LORD by fire.

The Grain Offering could be offered 'baked in the oven;' it could be offered 'baked in a pan,' i.e. griddle, or 'baked in a covered pan,' i.e. frying pan.

Now when you bring an offering of a grain offering baked in an oven, it shall be unleavened cakes of fine flour mixed with oil, or unleavened wafers spread with oil.

And if your offering is a grain offering made on the griddle, it shall be of fine flour, unleavened, mixed with oil; you shall break it into bits, and pour oil on it; it is a grain offering.

Now if your offering is a grain offering made in a pan, it shall be made of fine flour with oil.

When you bring in the grain offering which is made of these things to the LORD, it shall be presented to the priest and he shall bring it to the altar.

The priest then shall take up from the grain offering its memorial portion, and shall offer it up in smoke on the altar as an offering by fire of a soothing aroma to the LORD.

And the remainder of the grain offering belongs to Aaron and his sons: a thing most holy, of the offerings to the LORD by fire.

No grain offering, which you bring to the LORD, shall be made with leaven, for you shall not offer up in smoke any leaven..."
Leviticus 2:1-11 NASB

Several common and significant points of the grain offering:

- The grain offering would be of fine flour
- All grain offerings included pressed oil and frankincense
- All grain offerings must be unleavened
- All grain offerings must be seasoned with salt
- Only a small part of the grain offering was burned as a memorial
- The majority of a grain offering was presented to the priests

Salt in Grain Offerings

"Every grain offering of yours, moreover, you shall season with salt, so that the salt of the covenant of your God shall not be lacking from your grain offering; with all your offerings you shall offer with salt."
Leviticus 2:13 NASB

Salt in grain offerings signified loyalty to keep a promise. Several words associated with salt include 'preserve,' 'fidelity,' 'and permanence.'

Approximately 700 years after God instructed Moses of the significance of salt in grain offerings, King Abijah used the term 'covenant of salt' to illustrate the solidarity of the covenant the LORD God of Israel made with King David.

Then Abijah stood on Mount Zemaraim, which is in the hill country of Ephraim, and said, "Listen to me, Jeroboam and all Israel:"

"Do you not know that the LORD God of Israel gave the rule over Israel forever to David and his sons by a covenant of salt?"
2 Chronicles 13:4-5 NSAB

Approximately 300 years after Abijah, God informed Ezekiel that salt would be included in the offerings during the millennial kingdom.

Salt in the New Testament

And then Jesus spoke of salt several times to His disciples during His earthly ministry.

"You are the salt of the earth; but if the salt has become tasteless, how will it be made salty again? It is good for

nothing any more except to be thrown out and trampled under foot by men."
Matthew 5:13 NASB

Salt in this passage is from the Greek *halas* meaning in the present context, 'purity.' The disciples were to go out into the corrupt world and share the truth. 'Salt' used metaphorically in this context also signifies wisdom and prudence.

Then after Jesus' departure, His disciple Paul echoed Jesus' teaching.

"Conduct yourselves with wisdom toward outsiders, making the most of the opportunity.

Let your speech always be with grace, seasoned, as it were, with salt, so that you may know how you should respond to each person."
Colossians 4:5-6 NASB

Peace Offerings

The peace offering was a voluntary offering which represented fellowship and reconciliation between the one making the offering and God.

"Now if this offering is a sacrifice of peace offerings, if he is going to offer out of the herd, whether male or female, he shall offer it without defect before the LORD...

And he shall lay his hand on the head of his offering and slay it at the doorway of the tent of meeting, and Aaron's sons, the priests, shall sprinkle the blood around on the altar.

And from the sacrifice of the peace offerings, he shall present an offering by fire to the LORD, the fat that covers the entrails and all the fat that is on the entrails,

...and the two kidneys with the fat that is on them, which is on the loins, and the lobe of the liver, which he shall remove with the kidneys".
Leviticus 3:1-4 NASB

"And the priest shall offer them (fat) up in smoke on the altar as food, an offering by fire for a soothing aroma; all fat is the LORD's."
Leviticus 3:16 NASB

Fat was not to be eaten. It represented food to symbolize a friendly relationship between the one making the offering and God.

Then Moses expounded on the details of the priest's duties and benefits of the peace offering.

"Speak to the sons of Israel, saying, 'He who offers the sacrifice of his peace offerings to the LORD shall bring his offering to the LORD from the sacrifice of his peace offerings.

His own hands are to bring offerings by fire to the LORD. He shall bring the fat with the breast, that the breast may be presented as a wave offering before the LORD.

And the priest shall offer up the fat in smoke on the altar; but the breast shall belong to Aaron and is sons.

And you shall give the right thigh to the priest as a contribution from the sacrifices of your peace offerings.

The one among the sons of Aaron who offers the blood of the peace offerings and the fat, the right thigh shall be his as his portion.'"
Leviticus 7:29-33 NASB

Summary points on peace offerings include:

- The offering could be either male or female
- The offering could be from the herd or the flock
- The offering must be without defect (blemish)
- The offering was totally voluntary
- The one making the offering must lay his hand on the head of the animal and kill it
- Blood from the offered animal was sprinkled by the priests all around the altar
- All the fat was removed from the offering and burned
- Aaron and his sons were to enjoy the best of the meat of the offered as heave or wave offerings

Heave and wave offerings will be addressed in more detail later in this chapter.

Sin Offerings

Now we progress from voluntary offerings to mandatory offerings. Whereas, with the burnt offering, grain offering, and peace offering, the one making the offering exercised his free choice to worship his God.

A key word in describing a voluntary offering was 'if' which in the Hebrew *im* implies 'either' or 'whether.'

On the other hand, a significant word in describing a mandatory offering such as the sin offering is 'shall' which implies 'command' or 'determination.'

Another key aspect of the sin offering is that the sin was committed unintentionally.

The Book of Leviticus gives four examples of sin offerings committed by:

- High Priest
- The total congregation
- A ruler or leader
- The common individual

We'll examine each and then note the similarities and differences.

Sins by the Anointed Priest or the Whole Congregation

Then the LORD spoke to Moses, saying, "Speak to the sons of Israel, saying, 'If a person sins unintentionally in any of the things which the LORD has commanded not to be done, and commits any of them,

...if the anointed priest sins so as to bring guilt on the people, then let him offer to the LORD a bull without defect as a sin offering for the sin he has committed.

And he shall bring the bull to the doorway of the tent of meeting before the LORD, and he shall lay his hand on the head of the bull, and slay the bull before the LORD.

Then the anointed priest is to take some of the blood of the bull and bring it to the tent of meeting.'"
Leviticus 4:1-5 NASB

The tent of meeting is the holy place.

"...and the priest shall dip his finger in the blood, and sprinkle some of the blood seven times before the LORD, in front of the veil of the sanctuary."
Leviticus 4:6 NASB

The veil of the sanctuary is in front of the Most Holy Place.

"The priest shall also put some of the blood on the horns of the altar of fragrant incense which is before the LORD in the tent of meeting;

... and all the blood of the bull he shall pour out at the base of the altar of burnt offering which is at the doorway of the tent of meeting.

And he shall remove from it all the fat of the bull of the sin offering: the fat that covers the entrails, and all the fat which is on the entrails,

...and the two kidneys with the fat that is on them, which is on the loins, and the lobe of the liver, which he shall remove with the kidneys

... (just as it is removed from the ox of the sacrifice of peace offerings), and the priest is to offer them up in smoke on the altar of burnt offering."
Leviticus 4:7-10 NASB

"But the hide of the bull and all its flesh with its head and its legs and its entrails and its refuse,

...that is, all the rest of the bull, he is to bring out to a clean place outside the camp where the ashes are poured out, and burn it on wood with fire; where the ashes are poured out it shall be burned."
Leviticus 4:11-12 NASB

Several key points include:

- The anointed priest who sinned would offer a bull, lay his hand on the bull's head, and kill it
- The anointed priest would take some of the bull's blood and bring it to the tabernacle of meeting
- The priest would sprinkle some of the blood seven times before the veil in front of the Most Holy Place
- The priest would put some of the blood on the horns of the altar of incense before the Most Holy Place
- The remainder of blood would be taken out near the entrance of the tabernacle and poured at the base of the altar of burnt offering
- All of the fat would be removed from the bull and offered to God as a sweet aroma
- The meat of the bull that was slain was cut into pieces as described in the peace offering
- The priests could then eat the choice meat of the sin offering
- What was left of the bull, i.e. the hide and its flesh, its head and legs, entrails and refuse would be burned outside the camp

The instructions for the sin offering for the whole congregation were the same as for the sin offering for an anointed priest.

Sin Offering for a Ruler or Leader of the People

"When a leader sins and unintentionally does any one of all the things which the LORD God has commanded not to be done, and he becomes guilty,

...If his sin which he has committed is made known to him, he shall bring for his offering a goat, a male without defect.

And he shall lay his hand on the head of the male goat, and slay it in the place where they slay the burnt offering before the LORD; it is a sin offering.

Then the priest is to take some of the blood of the sin offering with his finger, and put it on the horns of the altar of burnt offering; and the rest of its blood he shall pour out at the base of the altar of burnt offering.

And all its fat he shall offer up in smoke on the altar in the case of the fat of the sacrifice of peace offerings. Thus the priest shall make atonement for him in regard to his sin, and he shall be forgiven."
Leviticus 4:22-26 NASB

There are several differences between the sin offering for a ruler and those for an anointed priest, or for the congregation at large.

- The ruler shall bring a male kid of the goats instead of a young bull
- The priest will put some of the blood of the kid on the horns of the altar of burnt offerings instead of the altar of incense

Sin Offering for the Common, Ordinary Citizen

"Now if anyone of the common people sins unintentionally in doing any of the things which the LORD has commanded not to be done, and becomes guilty,

...if his sin, which he has committed is made known to him, then he shall bring for his offering a goat, a female without defect, for his sin which he has committed.

And he shall lay his hand on the head of the sin offering, and slay the sin offering at the place of the burnt offering.

And the priest shall take some of its blood with his finger and put it on the horns of the altar of burnt offering; and all the rest of its blood he shall pour out at the base of the altar.

Then he shall remove all its fat, just as the fat was removed from the sacrifice of peace offerings; and the priest shall offer it up in smoke on the altar for a soothing aroma to the LORD.

Thus the priest shall make atonement for him, and he shall be forgiven."
Leviticus 4:27-31 NASB

The only difference between the sin offering for a ruler and a common person is the animal being offered. Whereas the ruler would offer a male kid of the goats for his sin offering, the common person would offer a female goat or lamb without defect for their sin offering.

For both the ruler and common person, the blood of the sacrifice would be sprinkled on the horns of the altar of burnt offering instead of within the holy place as was required for a priest or the congregation at large.

The Trespass (Guilt) Offering

While the Sin Offering dealt primarily with sins of commission, the Trespass Offering dealt primarily with sins of omission.

Even though the person might not have recognized certain words or actions as sin at the time, when he realized they constituted sin, it was his responsibility to bring it to light and make a trespass offering.

The following stresses what a person should have done, but didn't.

"Now if a person sins, after he hears a public adjuration to testify, when he is a witness, whether he has seen or otherwise known, if he does not tell it, then he will bear his guilt.

Or if a person touches any unclean thing, whether a carcass of an unclean beast, or the carcass of unclean cattle, or a carcass of unclean swarming things, though it is hidden from him, and he is unclean, then he will be guilty.

Or if he touches human uncleanness, of whatever sort his uncleanness may be with which he becomes unclean, and it is hidden from him, and then he comes to know it, he will be guilty.

Or if a person swears thoughtlessly with his lips to do evil or to do good, in whatever matter a man may speak thoughtlessly with an oath, and it is hidden from him, and then he comes to know it, he will be guilty in one of these.

So it shall be when he becomes guilty in one of these, that he shall confess that in which he has sinned.

He shall also bring his guilt offering to the LORD for his sin which he has committed, a female from the flock, a lamb or a goat as a sin offering. So the priest shall make atonement on his behalf for his sin."
Leviticus 5:1-6 NASB

Several summary thoughts:

- Even though the sin was unintentional, the trespass offering was mandatory
- The offering could be a female lamb from the flock, or a kid of the goats, or two turtledoves, or two young

pigeons, or flour without oil or frankincense, because it is a sin offering

- If the offering is two turtledoves or two young pigeons, one of them shall be a sin offering and the other shall be a burnt offering
- Some of the blood of the trespass offering shall be sprinkled on the side of the burnt altar and the remainder poured at the base of the altar
- The other, which served as a burnt offering, shall be completely burned up
- If the offering is flour, the priest shall take a handful and burn it on the altar, the remainder of the flour shall belong to the priest

Trespass (Guilt) Offerings with Restitution

If a person commits a trespass which harms holy things of the LORD, he must make restitution to the LORD. Likewise if a person commits a trespass which harms his neighbor's property, he must make restitution, plus make a trespass offering.

"If a person acts unfaithfully and sins unintentionally against the LORD's holy things, then he shall bring his guilt offering to the LORD:

...a ram without defect from the flock, according to your valuation in silver by shekels, in terms of the shekel of the sanctuary, for a guilt offering.

And he shall make restitution for that which he has sinned against the holy thing, and shall add to it a fifth part of it, and give it to the priest.

The priest shall then make atonement for him with the ram of the guilt offering, and it shall be forgiven him.

Now if a person sins and does any of the things which the LORD has commanded not to be done, though he was unaware, still he is guilty, and shall bear his punishment.

He is then to bring to the priest a ram without defect from the flock, according to your valuation, for a guilt offering so the priest shall make atonement for him concerning his error in which he sinned unintentionally and did not know it, and it shall be forgiven him.

It is a guilt offering; he was certainly guilty before the LORD."
Leviticus 5:15-19 NASB

Highlights of restitution required for harm done to holy things of the LORD.

- The offender must make restitution of one hundred and twenty percent of the harm done to the holy thing and present it to the priest
- The offender must also make a trespass offering in order to have the priest atone for his sin
- The trespass offering of the ram would be killed at the altar for burnt offerings

- The blood of the trespass offering would be sprinkled around on the altar of burnt offering
- All the fat from the offering would be removed and the priest would burn them on the altar as an offering made by fire to the LORD
- The trespass offering could be eaten by all the priests because it is like a sin offering; there is one law for both

The following applies to trespass offerings with restitution when a man consciously causes harm to his neighbor by being untruthful or deceitful.

"When a person sins and acts unfaithfully against the LORD, and deceives his companion in regard to a deposit or a security entrusted to him, or through robbery, or if he has extorted from his companion,

...or has found what was lost and lied about it and sworn falsely, so that he sins in regard to any one of the things a man may do;

...then it shall be, when he sins and becomes guilty, that he shall restore what he took by robbery, or what he got by extortion, or the deposit which was entrusted to him, or the lost thing which he found,

...or anything about which he swore falsely; he shall make restitution for it in full, and add to it one fifth more. He shall give it to the one to whom it belongs on the day he presents his guilt offering.

Then he shall bring to the priest his guilt offering to the LORD, a ram from the flock without defect, according to your valuation, for a guilt offering,

...and the priest shall make atonement for him before the LORD; and he shall be forgiven for any one of the things which he may have done to incur guilt."
Leviticus 6:2-7 NASB

- Sins committed against one's neighbor are indirectly sins against God
- The priest would set a value of the harm done
- The sinner must restore one hundred and twenty percent of the value of the harm done to one's neighbor, plus offer the trespass offering
- The offering for this type of sin is also a ram from the flock without blemish as described above

Dealing with Intentional Sins

The above sin offerings and trespass offerings were required for unintentional sins and sins against one's neighbor. The Old Testament also has much to say about dealing with presumptuous sins.

"But the person who does anything defiantly, whether he is native or an alien, that one is blaspheming the LORD; and that person shall be cut off from among his people (put to death).

Because he has despised the word of the LORD and has broken His commandment, that person shall be completely cut off; his guilt shall be on him."
Numbers 15:30-31 NASB

Accompanying Offerings

There were two offerings required to accompany the burnt and peace offerings. They are Grain Offerings and Drink (Libation) Offerings.

"Speak to the sons of Israel, and say to them, 'When you enter the land where you are to live, which I am giving you,

...then make an offering by fire to the LORD, a burnt offering or a sacrifice to fulfill a special vow, or as a freewill offering or in your appointed times, to make a soothing aroma to the LORD, from the herd or from the flock.

And the one who presents his offering shall present to the LORD a grain offering of one-tenth of an ephah of fine flour mixed with one-fourth of a hin of oil,

...and you shall prepare wine for the libation, one-fourth of a hin, with the burnt offering or for the sacrifice, for each lamb.'"
Numbers 15:2-5 NASB

Therefore, a grain offering and drink (libation) offering would accompany burnt offerings or peace offerings, for nearly any occasion.

"And when you prepare a bull as a burnt offering or a sacrifice, to fulfill a special vow, or for peace offerings to the LORD,

...then you shall offer with the bull a grain offering of three-tenths of an ephah of fine flour mixed with one-half a hin of oil;

...and you shall offer as the libation one-half a hin of wine as an offering by fire, as a soothing aroma to the LORD."
Numbers 15:8-10 NASB

The amount of flour and pressed oil of the grain offering, and the amount of wine of the drink offering would depend on the animal being offered, the purpose of the offering, or the appointed feast day being celebrated.

"Thus it shall be done for each ox, or for each ram, or for each of the male lambs, or of the goats.

According to the number that you prepare, so you shall do for everyone according to their number."
Numbers 15:11-12 NASB

Heave Offerings

Heave offerings reflect the way in which several of the primary offerings were to be presented.

Heave offering is from the Hebrew *Terumah* meaning a gift or oblation offered by raising it high in some given motion as it was placed on the altar.

"Speak to the sons of Israel, and say to them, 'When you enter the land where I bring you,

...then it shall be, that when you eat of the food of the land, you shall lift up an offering to the LORD.

Of the first of your dough you shall lift up a cake as an offering; as the offering of the threshing floor, so you shall lift it up.'"
Numbers 15:18-20 NASB

A heave offering, however, can also consist of a tithe received by the Levites.

"Moreover, you shall speak to the Levites and say to them, 'When you take from the sons of Israel the tithe which I have given you from them for your inheritance, then you shall present an offering (heave offering) from it to the LORD, a tithe of the tithe.

And your offering shall be reckoned (considered) to you as the grain from the threshing floor or the full produce from the wine vat.'"
Numbers 18:26-27 NASB

"And you shall say to them, 'When you have offered (heaved) from it the best of it, then the rest shall be reckoned

to the Levites as the product of the threshing floor, and as
the product of the wine vat (press).'"
Numbers 18:28-30 NASB

The phrase 'have offered' in the above is 'lifted' in the NKJV and originally found in the KJV as 'heaved' which means 'raise' or 'lift.'

The heave offering can also refer to the offering of meat from an animal being offered, such as in a peace offering.

The following illustrates that a wave offering can be used along with a heave offering.

The context is part of the consecration of Aaron and his sons.

"Then you shall take the breast of Aaron's ram of
ordination (consecration), and wave it as a wave offering
before the LORD; and it shall be your portion.

And you shall consecrate (sanctify) the breast of the
wave offering and the thigh of the heave offering which was
waved and which was offered from the ram of ordination
(consecration), from the one which was for Aaron and from
the one which was for his sons."
Exodus 29:26-27 NASB

Interestingly the word 'waved' in the above is 'raised' in the NKJV and 'heaved up' in the KJV.

Wave Offerings

Similar to heave offerings, a wave offering is a method of making a primary offering.

The Hebrew word for 'wave' is *nuph* which has synonyms including 'move' and 'shake.'

"For I have taken the breast of the wave offering and the thigh of the contribution from the sons of Israel from the sacrifices of their peace offerings, and have given them to Aaron the priest and to his sons as their due forever from the sons of Israel."
Leviticus 7:34 NASB

Therefore, Scripture reveals that both wave offerings and heave offerings were an integral part of the primary 'peace offering.'

A wave offering could also be gold.

"All the gold that was used for the work, in all the work of the sanctuary (holy place), even the gold of the wave offering, was 29 talents..."
Exodus 38:24 NASB

As the LORD spoke to Aaron regarding the duty of the priests and their reward for caring for the tabernacle, He said:

"This also is yours, the offering of their gift, even all the wave offerings of the sons of Israel; I have given them to you

and to your sons and daughters with you, as a perpetual allotment. Everyone of your household who is clean may eat it.

All the best of the fresh oil and all the best of the fresh wine and of the grain, the first fruits of those which they give to the LORD, I give them to you."
Numbers 18:11-12 NASB

Therefore, the best that was offered to God as heave and wave offerings were given back to the priests for their service.

Offerings in the Future

During the kingdom age following this present age and tribulation, numerous offerings will be made in the millennial temple.

The Bible lists the following offerings to be made during the millennial kingdom at such times as the New Moons, the Sabbaths, and at appointed seasons of the house of Israel, including Passover and Feast of Tabernacles. There will also be a sin offering beginning on the first day of the first month.

- Burnt offerings
- Peace offerings
- Grain offerings
- Drink offerings

- Sin offerings
- Trespass offerings

There will be a chief prince, and other princes, that will assist in administering the kingdom.

"And it shall be the prince's part to provide the burnt offerings, the grain offerings, and the drink offerings, at the feasts, on the new moons, and on the Sabbaths, at all the appointed feast of the house of Israel;

...he shall provide the sin offering, the grain offering, the burnt offering, and the peace offerings, to make atonement for the house of Israel."
Ezekiel 45:17 NASB

The specific feast celebrations to be observed in the millennial kingdom and their dates will be discussed in more detail in Chapter 2.

Chapter 2

Blood in Israel's Sacred Feast Days

Let's begin by examining the Hebrew calendar used to define the significant months and dates identifying specific feast days.

Month	Feast	Date or Dates
Abib/Nisan	Passover	14
	Unleavened Bread	15-21
	Firstfruits	16
Lyar		
Sivan	Feast of Weeks or Harvest (Pentecost) (50 days after Firstfruits)	6
Tammuz		
Av		
Elul		
Tishrei	Trumpets (Rosh Hashanah)	1-2
	Atonement (Yom Kippur)	10
	Tabernacles or Booths (Sukkot)	15-22
Cheshvan		
Kislev		
Tevet		
Shevat		
Adar		

Passover

The Passover was instituted on the night before the Exodus.

Pharaoh had been given one last chance to avoid the tenth and deadly plague.

Then Pharaoh said to him, "Get away from me! Beware, do not see my face again, for in the day you see my face you shall die!"

And Moses said, "You are right; I shall never see your face again!"
Exodus 10:28-29 NASB

And Moses said, "Thus says the LORD, 'About midnight I am going out into the midst of Egypt,

...and all the first-born in the land of Egypt shall die, from the first-born of Pharaoh who sits on his throne, even to the first-born of the slave girl who is behind the millstones; all the first-born of the cattle as well.'"
Exodus 11:4-5 NASB

Shortly before the night of the deadly plague, the LORD spoke to Moses and told him how to prepare for leaving Egyptian bondage. The meaning of the method that God used to spare His people from death would have everlasting effects.

God spoke the following to Moses and Aaron.

"This month shall be the beginning of months for you; it is to be the first month of the year to you."
Exodus 12:2 NASB

Then God gave the words to Moses and Aaron to 'speak to the congregation of Israel.'

"On the tenth of this month they are each one to take a lamb for themselves, according to their fathers' households, a lamb for each household.

Your lamb shall be an unblemished male a year old; you may take it from the sheep or from the goats.

And you shall keep it until the fourteenth day of the same month, then the whole assembly of the congregation of Israel is to kill it at twilight."
Exodus 12:3, 5-6 NASB

This is where an interpretative challenge enters. Many Jews interpreted 'twilight' to be the time before, but approaching sunset. While many others believe 'twilight' meant the time between sunset and darkness.

The KJV, in fact, uses the word 'evening' while the NKJV and NASB use 'twilight.' Evening is translated to mean dusk, or sundown.

For example, in Exodus 12:6 above, the NASB uses 'twilight,' while the KJV of Exodus 12:6 reads:

"And ye shall keep it up until the fourteenth day of the same month: and the whole assembly of the congregation of Israel shall kill it in the evening."
Exodus 12:6 KJV

But then, how significant is this difference? In either case, the Passover Lamb was killed on the fourteenth day of the first month of Abib/Nisan before dark.

The Passover Lamb was to be eaten with unleavened bread and bitter herbs on the same day that it was killed.

"And they shall eat the flesh that same night, roasted with fire, and they shall eat it with unleavened bread and bitter herbs."
Exodus 12:8 NASB

Unleavened bread will be covered in more detail when discussing the Feast of Unleavened Bread directly following the Passover Feast.

The Hebrew word used in this verse for bitter is *al* which is to call to mind the bitterness of the slavery and bondage experienced by the Israelites in Egypt. The bitterness was to be overpowered by the sweet flesh of the lamb.

How about the blood of the lamb that was slain?

"Moreover, they shall take some of the blood and put it on the two doorposts (side posts) and on the lintel (upper door post) of the houses in which they eat it."
Exodus 12:7 NASB

"...it is the LORD's Passover."
Exodus 12:11b NASB

Another requirement of the slain lamb was that none of its bones should be broken.

"...you are not to bring forth any of the flesh outside of the house, nor are you to break any bone of it."
Exodus 12:46 NASB

And then God revealed what He was going to do to the Egyptians.

"For I will go through the land of Egypt on that night, and will strike down all the first-born in the land of Egypt, both man and beast; and against all the gods of Egypt I will execute judgments – I am the LORD.

And the blood shall be a sign for you on the houses where you live; and when I see the blood I will pass over you, and no plague will befall you to destroy you when I strike the land of Egypt."
Exodus 12:12-13 NASB

Thus God redeemed His people from Egyptian bondage; they were saved by the blood of the Passover Lamb. The significance of that event would be everlasting.

"Now this day will be a memorial to you, and you shall celebrate it as a feast to the LORD; throughout your generations you are to celebrate it as a permanent ordinance."
Exodus 12:14 NASB

But did Israel faithfully keep the Passover throughout their generations?

They did for a while. Consider the words of Moses written just before the Israelites were to cross the Jordan to enter Canaan.

"Observe the month of Abib and celebrate the Passover to the LORD your God, for in the month of Abib the LORD your God brought you out of Egypt by night."
Deuteronomy 16:1 NASB

Joshua was also faithful to keep the Passover. The time was 1405 BC.

While the sons of Israel camped at Gilgal, they observed the Passover on the evening of the fourteenth day of the month on the desert plains of Jericho.
Joshua 5:10 NASB

Then it appears that there was a gap of approximately 300 – 400 years that the Passover was not kept.

King Hezekiah began his rule in 715 BC. He was a good king and restored temple worship and burnt offerings.

He also reinstated the Passover.

Now Hezekiah sent to all Israel and Judah and wrote letters also to Ephraim and Manasseh, that they should

come to the house of the LORD at Jerusalem to celebrate the Passover to the LORD God of Israel.
2 Chronicles 30:1 NASB

Less than a century after the reign of Hezekiah, King Josiah also ordered the Passover to be kept.

Then the king (Josiah) commanded all the people saying, "Celebrate the Passover to the LORD our God as it is written in this book of the covenant.

Surely such a Passover had not been celebrated from the days of the judges who judged Israel, nor in all the days of the kings of Israel and of the kings of Judah."

But in the eighteenth year of King Josiah, this Passover was observed to the LORD in Jerusalem.
2 Kings 23:21-23 NASB

The Babylonian captivity, and the destruction of Jerusalem, was near at hand.

After the 70 year captivity and the restoration of the temple, Ezra reinstated the Passover.

And the exiles observed the Passover on the fourteenth of the first month.
Ezra 6:19 NASB

It appears that the Passover was kept, with several interruptions, during the time of the Maccabees; during the time of Christ; up to the destruction of the temple in 70 AD.

The Fulfillment of Passover, and the Future of the Feast

Then came the day of Unleavened Bread on which the Passover lamb had to be sacrificed.

And He (Jesus) sent Peter and John, saying, "Go and prepare the Passover for us, that we may eat it."
Luke 22:7-8 NASB

And when the hour had come He reclined at the table, and the apostles with Him.

And He said to them, "I have earnestly desired to eat this Passover with you before I suffer;

...for I say to you, I shall never again eat it until it is fulfilled in the kingdom of God."
Luke 22:14-16 NASB

Paul subsequently commented on the Passover and its fulfillment.

"For Christ our Passover also has been sacrificed."
1 Corinthians 5:7b NASB

"Let us therefore celebrate the feast, not with old leaven nor with the leaven of malice and wickedness, but with the unleavened bread of sincerity and truth."
1 Corinthians 5:8 NASB

Thus, Christ was the true Passover Lamb, and the Passover feast will be reinstated in the future millennial kingdom.

Ezekiel received God's word relative to the future Passover 600 years before the true Passover Lamb was even born. God was telling Ezekiel what would happen in the future kingdom at the end of the great tribulation.

"In the first month, on the fourteenth day of the month, you shall have the Passover, a feast of seven days; unleavened bread shall be eaten."
Ezekiel 45:21 NASB

And lastly, when was it determined that Christ would be the Passover Lamb?

All who dwell on the earth will worship him (anti-Christ), whose names have not been written in the Book of Life of the Lamb slain from the foundation of the world.
Revelation 13:8 NKJV

The Feast of Unleavened Bread

The Feast of Unleavened Bread was one of the three feasts requiring all males to journey to Jerusalem to celebrate annually.

In the Bible, frequently the Passover and the seven days of Unleavened Bread are combined, i.e. sometimes they are both simply expressed as the Passover, and sometimes both are expressed as the Feast of Unleavened Bread.

There is also much disagreement as to whether the combined event is of seven day duration, or eight day duration.

It may depend on when a day is believed to start and when it ends. The same challenge was present at the time of Jesus, i.e. how could the Passover meal be eaten before the Lamb was slain?

In Jesus times, in the area around Galilee, a day was said to be from sunrise to sunrise. In the area around Jerusalem, where the pious Jews dwelt, a day was said to begin and end at sunset.

Recall that the Passover Lamb was killed at twilight on the fourteenth day of Abib/Nisan and eaten that same evening without leaven.

"And they shall eat the flesh that same night, roasted with fire, and they shall eat it with unleavened bread and bitter herbs."
Exodus 12:8 NASB

Now then, when did the Israelites leave their homes in Egypt to journey to the Promised Land?

"And you shall take a bunch of hyssop and dip it in the blood which is in the basin, and apply some of the blood

that is in the basin to the lintel and the two doorposts; and none of you shall go outside the door of his house until morning."
Exodus 12:22 NASB

'Morning' is from the Hebrew *'boqer'* meaning 'dawn' or 'morrow.'

Thus began the seven days Feast of Unleavened Bread.

"Seven days you shall eat unleavened bread, but on the first day you shall remove leaven from you houses; for whoever eats anything leavened from the first day until the seventh day, that person shall be cut off from Israel.

And on the first day you shall have a holy assembly, and another holy assembly on the seventh day; no work at all shall be done on them, except what must be eaten by every person, that alone may be prepared by you."
Exodus 12:15-16 NASB

'No work at all' means no occupational work. Preparing the food each day for the seven day celebration was exempted from the command.

"And you shall present an offering by fire, a burnt offering to the LORD; two bulls and one ram and seven male lambs one year old, having them without defect.

And for their grain offering, you shall offer fine flour mixed with oil; three-tenths of a measure (ephah) for a bull and two-tenths for the ram.

A tenth of a measure you shall offer for each of the seven lambs,

...and one male goat for a sin offering, to make atonement for you.

After this manner you shall present daily, for seven days..."
Numbers 28:19-22, 24a NASB

Recall:

"In the first month, on the fourteenth day of the month at evening, you shall eat unleavened bread, until the twenty-first day of the month at evening.

Seven days there shall be no leaven found in your houses..."
Exodus 12:18-19a NASB

Remember, the Israelites were not to begin their journey until the morning after the Passover Lamb was slain and eaten.

Therefore, let's count the days. Beginning with the fourteenth day through the twenty-first day is eight days. From the fifteenth day until the twenty-first day is seven days. Thus, the seven day Feast of Unleavened Bread begins on the fifteenth day of Abib/Nisan as confirmed by the following.

"These are the appointed times of the LORD, holy convocations which you shall proclaim at the times appointed for them.

In the first month, on the fourteenth day of the month at twilight is the LORD's Passover.

Then on the fifteenth day of the same month there is the Feast of Unleavened Bread to the LORD; for seven days you shall eat unleavened bread."
Leviticus 23:4-6 NASB

The Hebrew for unleavened is *marar* meaning that no yeast was added to the bread for several reasons; one reason was that to cause the bread to rise with yeast would consume valuable time.

Interestingly, several synonyms for *marar* include 'grieve, provoke, vex, and angry.'

There are varied opinions as to why unleavened bread was stressed. One popular opinion is that it was a reminder that the Hebrews left Egypt in a rush and didn't have time for baked bread to rise.

This opinion is supported by Scripture.

"You shall not eat leavened bread with it; seven days you shall eat with it unleavened bread, the bread of affliction (for you came out of the land of Egypt in haste),

...in order that you may remember all the days of your life the day when you came out of the land of Egypt."
Deuteronomy 16:3 NASB

The Hebrew word for affliction is *oniy* meaning 'depression,' 'misery,' or 'trouble.'

In the New Testament, the Greek word equivalent to *marar* was *azumos* which figuratively meant 'un-penetrated by evil.' This is the Greek word for unleavened found in the following which represented the sinlessness of Christ.

"...Do you not know that a little leaven leavens the whole lump of dough?

Let us therefore celebrate the feast, not with old leaven, nor with the leaven of malice and wickedness, but with the unleavened bread of sincerity and truth."
1 Corinthians 5:6, 8 NASB

Two other much used Greek words used for leaven are *zume* and *zumoo* meaning typically 'what did not belong originally and essentially to life, namely sin.'

...He began saying to His disciples first of all, "Beware of the leaven of the Pharisees, which is hypocrisy."
Luke 12:1b NASB

He spoke another parable to them, "The kingdom of heaven is like leaven, which a woman took, and hid in three pecks of meal, until it was all leavened."
Matthew 13:33 NASB

Jesus was explaining that the use of leaven by His enemies in this verse describes the permeating affect of false doctrine which distorts the doctrine of the kingdom of God.

And Jesus said to them, "Watch out and beware of the leaven of the Pharisees and Sadducees."

Then they understood that He did not say to beware of the leaven of bread, but of the teaching of the Pharisees and Sadducees.
Matthew 16:6, 12 NASB

Paul affirmed the negative affects of leaven on new believers.

"You were running well; who hindered you from obeying the truth?

This persuasion did not come from Him who calls you.

A little leaven leavens the whole lump of dough.

I have confidence in you in the Lord, that you will adopt no other view; but the one who is disturbing you shall bear his judgment, whoever he is."
Galatians 5:7-10 NASB

Of a surety, the effects of leaven will be overcome with the truth.

As mentioned in the previous section, when the Passover will be observed in the millennial kingdom, it will be a seven day event with unleavened bread eaten each day.

"In the first month, on the fourteenth day of the month, you shall have the Passover, a feast of seven days; unleavened bread shall be eaten."
Ezekiel 45:21 NASB

Feast of First Fruits

The Feast of First Fruits was celebrated on the 16th day of Abib/Nisan, or the second day of the Feast of Unleavened Bread.

The Feast of First Fruits was not to begin until Israel had taken possession of the Promised Land and began planting and harvesting.

God instructed Moses to speak to the children of Israel…

Then the LORD spoke to Moses, saying, "Speak to the sons of Israel, and say to them, 'When you enter the land which I am going to give to you and reap its harvest, then you shall bring in the sheaf of the first fruits of your harvest to the priest.

And he shall wave the sheaf before the LORD for you to be accepted; on the day after the Sabbath the priest shall wave it.'"
Leviticus 23:9-11 NASB

The sheaf consisted of a measure of grain bound as if to merchandise it. It was the first of the harvest, and no one was to eat any of the crop until after the first fruits were offered.

The Hebrew for 'first fruits' is *Reshith,* which meant not only first, but also 'best' or 'choice.'

The phrase 'on the day after the Sabbath' means the day after the Sabbath of the seven day Feast of Unleavened Bread, the fifteenth day of Abib/Nisan. The Feast of First Fruits then would be celebrated on the sixteenth day of Abib/Nisan.

The first fruits were to be given to the priests.

"Now this shall be the priests' due from the people...

... You shall give him the first fruits of your grain, your new wine, and your oil, and the first shearing of your sheep.

For the LORD your God has chosen him and his sons from all your tribes, to stand and serve in the name of the LORD forever."
Deuteronomy 18:3a, 4-5 NASB

There were other specific instructions to be followed when offering the first fruits of grain.

"Also if you bring a grain offering of early ripened things to the LORD, you shall bring fresh heads of grain roasted in the fire, grits of new growth, for the grain offering of your early ripened things.

You shall then put oil on it and lay incense on it; it is a grain offering.

And the priest shall offer up in smoke its memorial portion, part of its grits and its oil with all its incense as an offering by fire to the LORD."
Leviticus 2:14-16 NASB

And recall, a grain offering and drink offering accompanied burnt offerings.

"Its grain offering shall then be two-tenths of an ephah of fine flour mixed with oil, an offering by fire to the LORD for a soothing aroma, with its libation, a fourth of a hin of wine".
Leviticus 23:13 NASB

The offering of first fruits was a voluntary offering which would be a precursor to Christ being the first fruits raised from the grave.

"But now Christ has been raised from the dead, the first fruits of those who are asleep.

54

For since by a man came death, by a man also came the resurrection of the dead.

For as in Adam all die, so also in Christ all shall be made alive.

But each in his own order: Christ the first fruits, after that those who are Christ's at His coming."
1 Corinthians 15:20-23 NASB

And there are other references to first fruits in the New Testament.

"For if the first fruit is holy, the lump is also holy; and if the root is holy, so are the branches."
Romans 11:16 NKJV

The 'root' represents the patriarchs of Israel, i.e. Abraham, Isaac, Jacob and Judah.

Consider further:

"For we know that the whole creation groans and suffers the pains of childbirth together until now.

And not only this, but also we ourselves, having the first fruits of the Spirit, even we ourselves groan within ourselves, waiting eagerly for our adoption as sons, the redemption of our body."
Romans 8:22-23 NASB

The redeemed of Christ are the first to possess the fruit of the Spirit. Even we groan within ourselves because of our sinfulness awaiting our new bodies and eternal inheritance.

And then James concludes our discussion on 'first fruits.'

"Every good thing bestowed and every perfect gift is from above, coming down from the Father of lights, with whom there is no variation, or shifting shadow.

In the exercise of His will He brought us forth by the word of truth, so that we might be, as it were, the first fruits among His creatures."
James 1:17-18 NASB

The early church was the first fruits which represents a plentiful harvest of followers to come.

Feast of Weeks

The fourth of the appointed feasts in the Old Testament is most commonly referred to as the Feast of Weeks. The Feast of Weeks occurs in the third month on the Jewish calendar, or Sivan.

The Feast of Weeks is the second of three annual feasts that required all males to journey to God's chosen location, which subsequently was Jerusalem.

The Bible reveals that the Feast of Weeks was not originally known as such.

"Three times a year you shall celebrate a feast to Me...

You shall observe the Feast of Unleavened Bread; for seven days you are to eat unleavened bread, as I commanded you, at the appointed time in the month Abib...

Also you shall observe the Feast of the Harvest of the first fruits of your labors from what you sow in the field; also the Feast of the Ingathering at the end of the year when you gather in the fruit of your labors from the field."
Exodus 23:14-16 NASB

Thus the Feast of Weeks was originally known as Feast of Harvest.

The starting date of the Feast of Weeks is well defined.

"You shall also count for yourselves from the day after the sabbath, from the day when you brought in the sheaf of the wave offering; there shall be seven complete sabbaths.

You shall count fifty days to the day after the seventh sabbath; then you shall present a new grain offering to the LORD."
Leviticus 23:15-16 NASB

Seven sabbaths equals forty-nine days plus one day equals fifty days from the day of first fruits, which occurred on the sixteenth day of Nisan. Thus the date of the Feast of Weeks is the sixth day of the third month of Sivan.

Then it is revealed what is to be offered.

"You shall bring in from your dwelling places two loaves of bread for a wave offering, made of two-tenths of a bushel; they shall be of a fine flour, baked with leaven as first fruits to the LORD."
Leviticus 23:17 NASB

It is thought that perhaps leaven was baked into the bread to indicate that the word of God would be compromised before the feast would be fulfilled in Christ.

"Along with the bread, you shall present seven one year old male lambs without defect, and a bull of the herd, and two rams; they are to be a burnt offering to the LORD, with their grain offering and their libations, an offering by fire of a soothing aroma to the LORD."
Leviticus 23:18 NASB

The details of burnt offerings have been explained earlier.

"You shall also offer one male goat for a sin offering and two male lambs one year old for a sacrifice of peace offerings.

The priest shall then wave them with the bread of the first fruits for a wave offering with two lambs before the LORD; they are to be holy to the LORD for the priest."
Leviticus 23:19-20 NASB

Note the major components of this offering, i.e. it includes burnt offerings (including grain and drink offerings), sin offering, and peace offerings.

And remember, a wave offering to God is returned to the priests for their use.

"On this same day you shall make a proclamation as well; you are to have a holy convocation. You shall do no laborious work. It is to be a perpetual statute in all your dwelling places throughout your generations."
Leviticus 23:21 NASB

"When you reap the harvest of your land, moreover, you shall not reap to the very corners of your field, nor gather the gleaning of your harvest; you are to leave them for the needy and the alien. I am the LORD your God."
Leviticus 23:22 NASB

The provision of gleaning was an integral part of the story of Ruth.

When she rose to glean, Boaz commanded his servants, saying, "Let her glean even among the sheaves, and do not insult her.

And also you shall purposely pull out for her some grain from the bundles and leave it that she may glean, and do not rebuke her."
Ruth 2:15-16 NASB

From the Feast of Weeks to Pentecost

The Greek word for Pentecost is *pentekoste* meaning fiftieth, i.e. a fiftieth part. Pentecost was so named because the original feast was celebrated on the fiftieth day, counting from the second day of the Festival of Unleavened Bread.

It was recently discussed that at the original Feast of Weeks, a burnt offering was made that included 'the bread of the first fruits.'

Recall that James stated:

"In the exercise of His will He brought us forth by the word of truth, so that we might be, as it were, the first fruits among His creatures."
James 1:18 NASB

And then we stated that the early church was the first fruits which represent a plentiful harvest of followers to come.

Luke recorded Jesus' words on the day of His ascension. This was on the fortieth day after Christ's resurrection.

And gathering them together, He commanded them not to leave Jerusalem, but to wait for what the Father had promised, "Which," He said, "you heard of from Me;

...for John baptized with water, but you shall be baptized with the Holy Spirit not many days from now."
Acts 1:4-5 NASB

'Not many days from now' was just ten days. Ten days waiting plus forty days between Jesus' resurrection and ascension equals fifty days.

And when the day of Pentecost had come, they were all together in one place.

And suddenly there came from heaven a noise like a violent, rushing wind, and it filled the whole house where they were sitting.

And they were all filled with the Holy Spirit...
Acts 2:1-2, 4a NASB

Their receiving of the Holy Spirit was the fulfillment of the promise that Jesus had made to His disciples just several days before His death.

"And I will ask the Father, and He will give you another Helper, that He may be with you forever;

...that is the Spirit of truth..."
John 14:16-17a NASB

"When the Helper comes, whom I will send to you from the Father, that is the Spirit of truth, who proceeds from the Father, He will bear witness of me..."
John 15:26 NASB

The Feast of Weeks, exactly fifty days after the Feast of First Fruits, was fulfilled.

Feast of Trumpets

The feast of trumpets is the fifth appointed feast, and the first of three that have not as yet been fulfilled.

A brief synopsis of the feast is found in Leviticus.

Again the LORD spoke to Moses, saying,

..."Speak to the sons of Israel, saying, 'In the seventh month on the first of the month, you shall have a rest, a reminder (memorial) by blowing of trumpets, a holy convocation.

...You shall not do any laborious work, but you shall present an offering by fire to the LORD.'"
Leviticus 23:23-25 NASB

While the original description of the feast spoke of a given day, it was really a two day feast, i.e. the first and second day of the seventh month of Tishrei.

The reason for the two day event focused on the actual observation of the new moon. If there were witnesses to the new moon on the evening following the twenty-ninth day of the sixth month, i.e. Elul, and those witnesses came and reported they had observed the new moon on the first day of Tishrei, then all was fine.

If, however, the witnesses didn't come forward until the second day, then the feast would begin on the second day of Tishrei, and then retroactively include the first day, thus making a two day holiday.

There are also varied opinions among Jewish scholars as to what the Feast of Trumpets really signified.

Some say that, inasmuch as the feast was a memorial, it must bring to mind some past event. Many believe that the past event was God speaking to the people from Mount Sinai. God's message was the proclamation of the Ten Commandments.

God's presence at that unforgettable moment was accompanied with loud sounds of trumpets.

So it came about on the third day, when it was morning, that there were thunder and lightning flashes and a thick cloud upon the mountain and a very loud trumpet sound, so that all the people who were in the camp trembled.
Exodus 19:16 NASB

Others believe that the Feast of Trumpets speaks of God re-gathering His people from all corners of the earth.

More details are found in the Book of Numbers.

"Now in the seventh month, on the first day of the month, you shall also have a holy convocation; you shall do no laborious work. It will be to you a day for blowing trumpets."
Numbers 29:1 NASB

'Blowing trumpets' means 'joy, rejoice, and triumph.'

The Hebrew word for 'convocation' means 'assembly,' 'public meeting,' or 'congregation.'

"And you shall offer a burnt offering as a soothing aroma to the LORD: one bull, one ram, and seven male lambs one year old without defect;

...also their grain offering, fine flour mixed with oil, three-tenths of a measure for the bull, two-tenths for the ram, and one-tenth for each of the seven lambs.

And offer one male goat for a sin offering, to make atonement for you,

...besides the burnt offering of the new moon, and its grain offering, and continual (regular) burnt offering and its grain offering, and their libations, according to their ordinance for a soothing aroma, an offering by fire to the LORD."
Numbers 29:2-6 NASB

Those who believe that the feast signifies God's re-gathering of His people after the tribulation, the following support their thinking.

"...then the LORD your God will restore you from captivity, and have compassion on you, and will gather you again from all the people where the LORD has scattered you.

If your outcasts are at the ends of the earth, from there the LORD your God will gather you, and from there He will bring you back.

And the LORD your God will bring you into the land which your fathers possessed, and you shall possess it; and He will prosper you and multiply you more than your fathers."
Deuteronomy 30:3-5 NASB

This feast is also comprehensive, i.e. it includes a burnt offering accompanied with the customary grain and drink offering.

It also includes the sacrifice of a goat for 'atonement.'

Jesus also spoke of the re-gathering of His people.

"Then the sign of the Son of Man will appear in heaven... and they will see the Son of Man coming on the clouds of heaven...

...And He will send His angels with a great sound of a trumpet, and they will gather together His chosen ones from the four winds, from one end of heaven to the other."
Matthew 24:30-31 NKJV

And Paul subsequently spoke of God's raising His people with the sound of a trumpet.

"Behold, I tell you a mystery; we shall not all sleep (die), but we shall all be changed,

...in a moment, in the twinkling of an eye, at the last trumpet; for the trumpet will sound, and the dead will be raised imperishable, and we shall be changed.'
1 Corinthians 15:51-52 NASB

"For the Lord Himself will descend from heaven with a shout, with the voice of the archangel, and with the trumpet of God; and the dead in Christ shall rise first."
1 Thessalonians 4:16 NASB

In Judaism the Feast of Trumpets (Rosh Hashanah) begins a time of penitence lasting until the Day of Atonement (Yom Kippur) on the tenth day of the seventh month.

Day of Atonement

Atonement was offered in several feast days, as in the Feast of Trumpets just discussed.

The present discussion of the Day of Atonement will refer to a 'once a year' solemn event to atone for the sins of the High Priest, his family, the sanctuary, and all the people.

The procedure for the Day of Atonement is quite detailed; however, due to its significance we'll go through it step by step.

Subsequently, God gave specific instruction to Moses relative to the annual Day of Atonement.

And the LORD spoke to Moses, saying, "On exactly the tenth day of this seventh month is the day of atonement; it shall be a holy convocation for you, and you shall humble (afflict) your souls and present an offering by fire to the LORD.

Neither shall you do any work on this same day, for it is a day of atonement, to make atonement on your behalf before the LORD your God."
Leviticus 23:26-28 NASB

The High Priest was the main participant in the annual Day of Atonement convocation.

Aaron began to prepare for his duty by cleansing himself with water. There was a bronze basin between the altar of burnt sacrifice and the tabernacle of meeting. It was here that Aaron washed. If Aaron or his sons did not obey this command, they would die.

Therefore, before donning the High Priest's clothing, Aaron washed himself.

"Therefore he shall wash his body in water, and put them on."
Leviticus 16:4b NKJV

Then after washing himself, he put on the High Priest's attire.

"He shall put the holy linen tunic and the linen trousers on his body; he shall be girded with a linen sash, and with the linen turban he shall be attired. These are holy garments."
Leviticus 16:4a NKJV

There were three different animals to be sacrificed.

"Thus Aaron shall come into the Holy Place: with the blood of a young bull as a sin offering, and of a ram as a burnt offering...And he shall take from the congregation of the children of Israel two kids of the goats as a sin offering..."
Leviticus 16:3, 5a NKJV

Aaron first offers the young bull as a sin offering for himself and his family.

"Aaron shall offer the bull as a sin offering, which is for himself, and make atonement for himself and for his house...

...and Aaron shall bring the bull of the sin offering...and shall kill the bull..."
Leviticus 16:6, 11 NKJV

Aaron would then take his hands full of incense and put it on the altar of incense before the veil.

"And he shall put the incense on the fire before the LORD, that the cloud of incense may cover the mercy seat that is on the Testimony, lest he die."
Leviticus 16:13 NKJV

Then Aaron would enter the Most Holy Place.

"Then he shall take a censer full of burning coals of fire from the altar before the LORD, with his hands full of sweet incense beaten fine, and bring it inside the veil...

...He shall take some of the blood of the bull and sprinkle it with his finger on the mercy seat on the east side; and before the mercy seat he shall sprinkle some of the blood with his finger seven times."
Leviticus 16:12, 14 NKJV

Aaron would then present two young goats to the LORD.

"He shall take the two goats and present them before the LORD at the door of the tabernacle of meeting...

...Then Aaron shall cast lots for the two goats: one lot for the LORD and the other lot for the scapegoat...

...And Aaron shall bring the goat on which the LORD's lot fell, and offer it as a sin offering...

...But the goat on which the lot fell to be the scapegoat shall be presented alive before the LORD, to make

atonement upon it, and to let it go as the scapegoat into the wilderness."
Leviticus 16:7-10 NKJV

Then Aaron would kill the goat for the sin offering.

"Then he shall kill the goat of the sin offering which is for the people, bring its blood inside the veil...

...do with that blood as he did with the blood of the bull, and sprinkle it on the mercy seat and before the mercy seat."
Leviticus 16:15 NKJV

The goat sin offering was not only for the people, but also for the Holy Place itself.

"So he shall make atonement for the Holy Place, because of the uncleanness of the children of Israel, and because of their transgressions, for all their sins; and so he shall do for the tabernacle of meeting which remains among them in the midst of their uncleanness."
Leviticus 16:16 NKJV

The law included that no other man would be in the tabernacle of meeting when the High Priest was in the Most Holy Place.

"There shall be no man in the tabernacle of meeting when he goes in to make atonement in the Holy Place, until

he comes out, that he may make atonement for himself, for his household, and for all the assembly of Israel."
Leviticus 16:17 NKJV

Then Aaron would exit the Most Holy Place and make atonement for the altar of incense before the veil.

"And he shall go out to the altar that is before the LORD, and make atonement for it, and shall take some of the blood of the bull and some of the blood of the goat, and put it on the horns of the altar all around...

...Then he shall sprinkle some of the blood on it with his finger seven times, cleanse it, and consecrate it from the uncleanness of the children of Israel."
Leviticus 16:18-19 NKJV

After Aaron leaves the Most Holy Place and the Holy Place, he consecrates the scapegoat.

"And when he has made an end of atoning for the Holy Place, the tabernacle of meeting, and the altar, he shall bring the live goat...

...Aaron shall lay both his hands on the head of the live goat, confess over it all the iniquities of the children of Israel, and all their transgressions, concerning all their sins, putting them on the head of the goat...

...and shall send it away into the wilderness by the hand of a suitable man...

...The goat shall bear on itself all their iniquities to an uninhabited land; and he shall release the goat in the wilderness."
Leviticus 16:20-22 NKJV

Then Aaron will return to the tabernacle, remove his High Priest attire, wash himself again and put on his regular priestly attire.

"Then Aaron shall come into the tabernacle of meeting, shall take off the linen garments which he put on when he went into the Holy Place, and shall leave them there...

...And he shall wash his body with water in a holy place, put on his garments, come out..."
Leviticus 16:23-24a NKJV

Aaron will then offer the burnt offering for the people.

"...and offer his burnt offering and the burnt offering of the people, and make atonement for himself and for the people."
Leviticus 16:24b NKJV

Then Aaron will burn the fat of the bull which was offered as a sin offering.

"The fat of the sin offering he shall burn on the altar."
Leviticus 16:25 NKJV

The man who released the scapegoat must also wash his clothes and bathe himself so he can re-enter the camp.

"And he who released the goat as the scapegoat shall wash his clothes and bathe his body in water, and afterward he may come into the camp."
Leviticus 16:26 NKJV

And as required for sin offerings, the remains of the sacrifices shall be removed from the camp.

"The bull for the sin offering and the goat for the sin offering, whose blood was brought in to make atonement in the Holy Place, shall be carried outside the camp. And they shall burn in the fire their skins, their flesh, and their offal."
Leviticus 16:27 NKJV

Likewise, he who burned them must wash so as to be able to return to the camp.

"Then he who burns them shall wash his clothes and bathe his body in water, and afterward he may come into the camp."
Leviticus 16:28 NKJV

"This shall be a statute forever for you: in the seventh month, on the tenth day of the month, you shall afflict your souls, and do no work at all...

...for on that day the priest shall make atonement for you, to cleanse you, that you may be clean from all your sins before the LORD."
Leviticus 16:29-30 NKJV

Let's summarize the activities of the High Priest on the Day of Atonement and then present the ultimate fulfillment of that sacred day.

- Aaron would wash himself and don the High Priest's attire
- Aaron would offer a bull as a sin offering for himself and his family
- Aaron would offer incense so that the cloud of incense would cover the mercy seat in the Most Holy place
- Aaron would take a censer of burning coals and some blood of the bull into the Most Holy place
- Aaron would sprinkle some of the blood on the mercy seat and in front of the mercy seat
- Aaron would take the goat offered for the sins of the people and do with the blood as he did with the blood of the bull
- Aaron would make atonement for the altar of incense with the blood of the bull and goat
- Aaron would place his hands on the scapegoat and send it away into the wilderness
- Then Aaron would remove his High Priestly garments, wash himself again, and put on regular priestly garments
- Then Aaron would offer the burnt offering for himself and the people on the altar of burnt sacrifice

Atonement in the above is from the Hebrew word *Kaphar* with several significant synonyms including 'mercy,' 'reconcile,' 'forgive,' and 'pardon.'

Likewise, 'mercy seat' in the above is from the Hebrew word *Kapporeth* meaning the golden cover of the Ark of the Covenant, and the place and object of propitiation. Propitiation is from the Hebrew word *hilasmos* meaning 'to pay the necessary price.'

God's justice demands that sin must be paid for by death, confirmed by the shedding of blood.

All is well except as noted earlier:

"For it is not possible that the blood of bulls and goats could take away sins."
Hebrews 10:4 NKJV

And while Aaron, as the High Priest, sacrificed an animal chosen by people, Jesus was both High Priest and the sacrifice chosen by God.

We'll list several New Testament passages that illustrate 'atonement.'

"For when we were still without strength, in due time Christ died for the ungodly."
Romans 5:6 NKJV

'Christ died for the ungodly' defines atonement.

"Now all things are of God, who has reconciled us to Himself through Jesus Christ..."
2 Corinthians 5:18 NKJV

'…reconciled us to Himself' defines atonement.

"Grace to you and peace from God the Father and our Lord Jesus Christ, who gave Himself for our sins, that He might deliver us from this present evil age…"
Galatians 1:3-4 NKJV

'…who gave Himself for our sins' defines atonement.

"Christ has redeemed us from the curse of the law, having become a curse for us…"
Galatians 3:13 NKJV

'Christ has redeemed us from the curse of the law' defines atonement.

"…so Christ was offered once to bear the sins of many."
Hebrews 9:28 NKJV

'…offered once to bear the sins…' defines atonement.

"…who Himself bore our sins in His own body on the tree…"
1 Peter 2:24 NKJV

'…bore our sins in His own body' defines atonement.

"For Christ also suffered once for sins, the just for the unjust, that He might bring us to God…"
1 Peter 3:18 NKJV

'...suffered once for sins...that He might bring us to God' defines atonement.

"And He Himself is the propitiation for our sins, and not for ours only but also for the whole world."
1 John 2:2 NKJV

'...He Himself is the propitiation for our sins' defines atonement.

Much more relative to Christ being High Priest and Mediator will be covered in chapter 4.

The Feast of Tabernacles

The Feast of Tabernacles is the last of the seven original feasts given to the Israelites while in the wilderness prior to entering the Promised Land.

"Three times you shall keep a feast to Me in the year: You shall keep the Feast of Unleavened Bread...as I commanded you...and the Feast of Harvest (Feast of Weeks)...and the Feast of Ingathering (Tabernacles) at the end of the year..."
Exodus 23:14-16 NKJV

Then specific details were given to Moses about the Feast of Tabernacles.

Then the LORD spoke to Moses, saying, "Speak to the children of Israel, saying: 'The fifteenth day of this seventh

month shall be the Feast of Tabernacles for seven days to the LORD."'
Leviticus 23:33-34 NKJV

"On the first day there shall be a holy convocation (Sabbath-rest). You shall do no customary work on it...

...For seven days you shall offer an offering made by fire to the LORD...

...On the eighth day you shall have a holy convocation..."
Leviticus 23:35-36 NKJV

Then they are told to build booths from branches in remembrance of God's provision and care during the wilderness years.

"And you shall take for yourselves on the first day the foliage of beautiful trees, branches of palm trees, the boughs of leafy trees, and willows of the brook; and you shall rejoice before the LORD your God for seven days...

...It shall be a statute forever in your generations...

...You shall dwell in booths (tabernacles-shelters made of boughs) that your generations may know that I made the children of Israel dwell in booths when I brought them out of the land of Egypt..."
Leviticus 23:40-43 NKJV

There were to be several different offerings and sacrifices on each of the seven days plus the eighth day, which would also be a sacred assembly.

The Feast of Tabernacles would include burnt, sin, grain and drink offerings.

"You shall present a burnt offering, an offering made by fire as a sweet aroma to the LORD: thirteen young bulls, two rams, and fourteen lambs in their first year. They shall be without blemish."
Numbers 29:13 NKJV

And grain offerings were to accompany the burnt offerings.

"Their grain offering shall be of fine flour mixed with oil: three-tenths of an ephah for each of the thirteen bulls, two-tenths for each of the two rams, and one-tenth for each of the fourteen lambs..."
Numbers 29:14 NKJV

Also on the first day of the feast, a kid of a goat would be offered as a sin offering. All these offerings would be in addition to the regular offerings of each day.

"...also one kid of the goats as a sin offering, besides the regular burnt offering, its grain offering, and its drink offering."
Numbers 29:16 NKJV

From the first day through the seventh day, the offerings would be nearly exactly the same, except there would be one less bull offered each day. For example, on the second day there would be twelve bulls offered instead of the thirteen offered on day one.

However, each day of the seven would include two rams and fourteen lambs for burnt offerings, and a kid of the goats for sin offering each of the seven days. The daily grain and drink offerings would remain the same per animal, but the daily total would reflect the decrease of one bull each day.

For example, consider the third day of the feast.

"On the third day present eleven bulls, two rams, fourteen lambs in their first year without blemish, and their grain offering and their drink offerings for the bulls, for the rams, and for the lambs, by their number, according to the ordinance; also one goat as a sin offering, besides the regular burnt offering, its grain offering, and its drink offering."
Numbers 29:20-22 NKJV

Day eight would again be a sacred assembly day, plus specific offerings.

"On the eighth day you shall have a sacred assembly. You shall do no customary work...

...You shall present a burnt offering, an offering made by fire as a sweet aroma to the LORD: one bull, one ram, seven lambs in their first year without blemish...

...and their grain offering and their drink offerings for the bull, for the ram, and for the lambs, by their number according to the ordinance...

...also one goat as a sin offering, besides the regular burnt offering, its grain offering, and its drink offering." Numbers 29:35-38 NKJV

Feasts and Offerings in the Millennial Kingdom

Approximately 820 years after the Feast of Tabernacles was initiated, Ezekiel wrote of that feast being celebrated in the millennial kingdom, along with other feasts and offerings.

To begin with, it will be noted that the first of the three feasts to be celebrated in the millennial kingdom is not the Passover (Unleavened Bread) as in days of old, but rather a seven day sin offering beginning on the first day of the first month.

"In the first month, on the first day of the month, you shall take a young bull without blemish and cleanse the sanctuary...

...The priest shall take some of the blood of the sin offering and put it on the doorposts of the temple, on the

four corners of the ledge of the altar, and on the gateposts of the gate of the inner court...

...And so you shall do on the seventh day of the month for every one who has sinned unintentionally or in ignorance. Thus you shall make atonement for the temple."
Ezekiel 45:18-20 NKJV

Then, in addition to the New Year sin offering beginning on the first day of the first month; the Passover, (Unleavened Bread) will also be observed in the first month.

"In the first month, on the fourteenth day of the month, you shall observe the Passover, a feast of seven days; unleavened bread shall be eaten.

And on that day the prince shall prepare for himself and for all the people of the land a bull for a sin offering.

On the seven days of the feast he shall prepare a burnt offering to the LORD, seven bulls and seven rams without blemish, daily for seven days...

...and a kid of the goats daily for a sin offering.

And he shall prepare a grain offering of one ephah for each bull and one ephah for each ram, together with a hin of oil for each ephah."
Ezekiel 45:21-22 NKJV

It is interesting to note that the animals offered in the millennial Passover/Unleavened offering are more than in the original Passover/Unleavened feast.

For example in the original feast there were two bulls, one ram, seven lambs, and one goat offered daily.

However, in the millennial feast there will be one bull offered as a sin offering on the first day, and seven bulls and seven rams for a burnt offering daily, and one kid of the goats offered each day for a sin offering.

Also there will be much more grain and drink offerings for each animal in the millennial kingdom than in the original.

That covers the Passover and Unleavened Bread. Then the Feast of Tabernacles is observed and celebrated in the kingdom.

"In the seventh month, on the fifteenth day of the month, at the feast, he shall do likewise for seven days, according to the sin offering, the burnt offering, the grain offering, and the oil."
Ezekiel 45:25 NKJV

And then about eighty years after Ezekiel, Zechariah affirmed the importance of the Feast of Tabernacles during the millennial kingdom.

"And it shall come to pass that everyone who is left of all the nations which came against Jerusalem shall go up from year to year to worship the King, the LORD of hosts, and to keep the Feast of Tabernacles...

...And it shall be that whichever of the families of the earth do not come up to Jerusalem to worship the king, the LORD of hosts, on them there will be no rain."
Zechariah 14:17 NKJV

Other Offerings in the Millennial Kingdom

Thus the major appointed feasts to be observed in the kingdom include:

- The New Year Sin Offering
- The Passover (Unleavened Bread) Feast
- The Feast of Tabernacles

However, there will be many other offerings made in the kingdom.

For example:

"Likewise the people of the land shall worship at the entrance to the gateway before the LORD on the Sabbaths and the New Moons."
Ezekiel 46:3 NKJV

"The burnt offering that the prince offers to the LORD on the Sabbath day shall be six lambs without blemish; and a ram without blemish;

... and the grain offering shall be one ephah for a ram, and the grain offering for the lambs, as much as he wants to give, as well as a hin of oil with every ephah."
Ezekiel 46:4-5 NKJV

And then for the New Moons:

"On the day of the New Moon it shall be a young bull without blemish, six lambs, and a ram; they shall be without blemish.

He shall prepare a grain offering of an ephah for a bull, an ephah for a ram, as much as he wants to give for the lambs, and a hin of oil with every ephah."
Ezekiel 46:6-7 NKJV

Also during that time, voluntary burnt or voluntary peace offerings will be made spontaneously.

"Now when the prince makes a voluntary burnt offering or voluntary peace offering to the LORD...he shall prepare his burnt offering and his peace offerings as he did on the Sabbath day."
Ezekiel 46:12 NKJV

And very significantly, there will be daily offerings.

"Thou shalt daily prepare a burnt offering unto the LORD of a lamb of the first year without blemish: thou shall prepare it every morning.

And thou shalt prepare a meat (grain) offering for it every morning, the sixth part of an ephah, and the third part of a hin of oil, to temper with the fine flour;

... a meat offering continually by a perpetual ordinance unto the LORD."
Ezekiel 46:13-14 KJV

The Hebrew word for 'continually' is *Tamidh* meaning 'without interruption,' and is also synonymous with 'perpetual.'

Likewise the Hebrew word for 'perpetual' above is *Olam* which means 'without end,' or 'eternal.'

Daily Offerings between now and the Millennial Kingdom

All indications are that there will be a temple and temple services restored and reinstated at or before the great tribulation.

The anti-Christ will originally allow that in his peacemaking efforts, but will subsequently put an end to such.

The prophet Daniel revealed the intentions of the anti-Christ several times.

"He shall speak pompous words against the Most High, shall persecute the saints of the Most High...

...and shall intend to change times and laws..."
Daniel 7:25 KJV

The Hebrew word for 'times' is *Zeman* meaning 'seasons' and 'appointed times.'

Daniel subsequently revealed the removal of the daily sacrifices during the mid-point of the tribulation.

"And from the time that the daily sacrifice shall be taken away, and the abomination that maketh desolate set up, there shall be a thousand two hundred and ninety days."
Daniel 12:11 KJV

However, during the millennial kingdom, Satan's puppets will be in the lake of fire, and he, himself will be confined to the bottomless pit during that thousand years.

During that time the kingdom feasts and offerings will be celebrated as revealed by Ezekiel.

Chapter 3

Blood in Ratifying Covenants

Let's begin with God's calling to Abram to leave his homeland to cross over the Euphrates River to a new land.

Now the LORD said to Abram, "Go forth from your country, and from your relatives and from your father's house, to the land which I will show you;

...and I will make you a great nation, and I will bless you, and make your name great; and so you shall be a blessing;

...and I will bless those who bless you, and the one who curses you I will curse. And in you all the families of the earth shall be blessed."
Genesis 12:1-3 NASB

The Abrahamic Covenant and its Unilateral Ratification

The above was an unconditional promise that God made to Abram, and God included this promise in the covenant that He subsequently unilaterally ratified with Abram.

Notice God's sovereignty in the above passage.

- To a land that I will show you
- I will make you a great nation

- I will bless you
- I will bless those who bless you
- The one who curses you I will curse

Abram inquired of God about his descendants, seeing that he and his wife were aging and they had no sons. God told Abram that he and his wife Sarai would have a son, and their descendants would be numbered as the stars in heaven.

Then God gave details of the land that He was giving Abram and his offspring.

As the covenant was to be ratified, God said:

"Bring Me a three year old heifer, and a three year old female goat, and a three year old ram, and a turtledove, and a young pigeon."

Then he brought all these to Him and cut them in two, and laid each half opposite the other; but he did not cut the birds.
Genesis 15:9-10 NASB

Therefore, the covenant God was going to make with Abram included the sacrifice of animals; blood was shed.

Then as twilight appeared, Abram fell into a deep sleep.

And it came about when the sun had set, that it was very dark, and behold, there appeared a smoking oven and a flaming torch which passed between these pieces.

On that day the LORD made a covenant with Abram, saying, "To your descendants I have given this land, from the river of Egypt as far as the great river, the river Euphrates..."
Genesis 15:17-18 NASB

It is very significant that the land promised to Abram and his descendants extends much further east than the land defining present day Israel.

Inasmuch as Abram was in a deep sleep, the covenant was ratified by God alone. Therefore, the covenant was unconditional and immutable.

The remainder of the Bible is based on God's unconditional promise and unilateral covenant with Abram.

Subsequent References to the Abrahamic Covenant

The Psalmist referred to the Abrahamic covenant while writing about God's eternal faithfulness.

He has remembered His covenant forever, the word which He commanded to a thousand generations,

... the covenant which He made with Abraham, and His oath to Isaac.

Then He confirmed it to Jacob for a statute, to Israel as an everlasting covenant, saying,

...*"To you I will give the land of Canaan as the portion of your inheritance..."*
Psalm 105:9-11 NASB

The prophet Zechariah spoke of God's covenant with Abraham which He ratified by himself with the shedding of blood. Zechariah was describing Israel's freedom because of the covenant.

"As for you also, because of the blood of My covenant with you, I have set your prisoners free..."
Zechariah 9:11 NASB

And then five hundred years after Zechariah the prophet, Zacharias, the father of John the Baptist, prophesied about the future of his son in relation to the Messiah.

"As He (God) spoke by the mouth of His holy prophets, who have been since the world began...

... that we should be saved from our enemies and from the hand of all who hate us, to perform the mercy promised to our fathers and to remember His holy covenant, the oath which He swore to our father Abraham..."
Luke 1:70-73 NKJV

Another Significant Covenant Ratified by Blood after the Exodus

Just prior to God's giving the Ten Commandments from Mount Sinai, God told Moses to consecrate the people and be prepared for a significant event that would occur three days later.

"...and let them be ready for the third day, for on the third day the LORD will come down on Mount Sinai in the sight of all the people."
Exodus 19:11 NASB

The people were not actually going to see God, rather they would see, or experience His presence, in a cloud of fire and smoke.

So it came about on the third day, when it was morning, that there were thunder and lightning flashes and a thick cloud upon the mountain and a very loud trumpet sound, so that all the people who were in the camp trembled.

Now Mount Sinai was all in smoke because the LORD descended upon it in fire; and its smoked ascended like the smoke of a furnace, and the whole mountain quaked violently.
Exodus 19:16, 18 NASB

Then God spoke the Ten Commandments in the hearing of the people.

And all the people perceived the thunder and the lightning flashes and the sound of the trumpet and the mountain smoking; and when the people saw it, they trembled and stood at a distance.

Then they said to Moses, "Speak to us yourself and we will listen; but let not God speak to us, lest we die."
Exodus 20:18-19 NASB

The people were very frightened because of God's magnificent presence.

They asked Moses to be their mediator between them and God.

Shortly thereafter the LORD said to Moses:

"Thus you shall say to the sons of Israel, 'You yourselves have seen that I have spoken to you from heaven.

You shall make an altar of earth for Me, and you shall sacrifice on it your burnt offerings and your peace offerings, your sheep and your oxen; in every place where I cause My name to be remembered, I will come to you and bless you.'"
Exodus 20:22, 24 NASB

This was not the first mention of burnt and peace offerings; such were offered by Noah and Abraham many years earlier.

Shortly after the Ten Commandments were given, God called to Moses and relayed in detail other commands and judgments.

And Moses wrote all the words of the LORD. And he rose early in the morning, and built an altar at the foot of the mountain, and twelve pillars according to the twelve tribes of Israel...

...Then he sent young men of the children of Israel, who offered burnt offerings and sacrificed peace offerings of oxen to the LORD...

...And Moses took half the blood and put it in basins, and half the blood he sprinkled on the altar...

...Then he took the Book of the Covenant and read in the hearing of the people...

...And they said, "All that the LORD has said we will do, and be obedient..."

...And Moses took the blood, sprinkled it on the people, and said, "This is the blood of the covenant which the LORD has made with you according to all these words."
Exodus 24:4-8 NKJV

This was before the tabernacle was constructed.

This covenant was extremely significant, i.e. it was ratified with blood from special burnt offerings by the people who had just said that they would fully obey God's commandments.

Plans for the Earthly Tabernacle to be patterned after the Heavenly

Shortly after the law was given, God gave instructions for the tabernacle which was completed in the first month of the second year after the Exodus.

The priests were consecrated before the tabernacle was completed, so they were ready to serve in the tabernacle as soon as it was finished.

The tabernacle of meeting was 150 ft x 75 ft. The opening to the tabernacle faced east. There were basically three parts to the tabernacle, i.e. outer court, the holy place, and the Most Holy Place.

Closest to the door of the tabernacle in the outer court was the altar of burnt offering. Between the altar of burnt offerings and the holy place was the bronze laver for washing.

The tabernacle itself measured 45 ft x 15 ft x 15 ft. The holy place measured 30 ft x 15 ft x 15 ft while the Most Holy Place was a cube, 15 ft x 15 ft x 15 ft.

Within the holy place were the Table of Showbread, the Golden Lampstand, and the Altar of Incense.

Within the Most Holy Place was the Ark of the Covenant, covered by the Mercy Seat.

There was a curtain in front of the holy place and a veil separating the holy place from the Most Holy Place.

Aaron and his Sons were consecrated with Blood in Preparation to serve in the Tabernacle

God gave Moses detailed instructions for the consecration ceremony. Not only did Moses relay the instructions to Aaron and his sons; he himself was very active in the consecration ceremony.

Thus God told Moses:

- Take a young bull and two rams
- Take unleavened bread, cakes, and wafers anointed with oil
- Bring Aaron and his sons to the entrance of the tabernacle of meeting
- Wash them with water in the Bronze Laver
- Dress Aaron with the clothes of the High Priest
- Dress Aaron's sons with the clothes of a priest

"Then you (Moses) shall bring the bull before the tent of meeting, and Aaron and his sons shall lay their hands on the head of the bull.

And you shall slaughter the bull before the LORD at the doorway of the tent of meeting."
Exodus 29:10-11 NASB

- Moses was told to take some of the blood and put it on the horns of the altar
- The remainder of the blood was to be poured out at the base of the altar
- All the fat was to be removed from the bull and burned on the altar
- The flesh and skin of the bull with its offal shall be burned outside the camp as a sin offering

"You (Moses) shall also take the one ram, and Aaron and his sons shall lay their hands on the head of the ram; and you shall slaughter the ram and shall take its blood and sprinkle it around on the altar."
Exodus 29:15-16 NASB

- Then Moses was to cut the ram in pieces and wash its entrails and legs
- Then the whole ram was to burned on the altar as a burnt offering
- This was to be a sweet aroma, made by fire, to the LORD

"Then you shall take the other ram, and Aaron and his sons shall lay their hands on the head of ram."
Exodus 29:19-20a NASB

- You shall put some of the blood on Aaron's right ear and on the right ears of his sons
- You shall put some of the blood on their right hand and on the big toe of their right foot

- You shall sprinkle the blood all around of the altar
- You shall take some of the blood, and some of the anointing oil and sprinkle it on Aaron and on his garments, on his sons and on the garments of his sons with him

So Moses took some of the anointing oil and some of the blood which was on the altar, and sprinkled it on Aaron, on his garments, on his sons, and on the garments of his sons with him; and he consecrated Aaron, his garments, and his sons, and the garment of his sons with him.
Leviticus 8:30 NASB

- Then take the fat of the ram, its right thigh, one loaf of bread, one cake made with oil, and one wafer of unleavened bread...
- Aaron and his sons will offer these as a wave offering
- Then you shall take these same components and burn them as a burnt offering
- Then you shall take the breast of the ram and offer it as a wave offering
- The thigh of the ram will be offered as a heave offering
- Thus, the thigh and breast, which are free from fat, shall become the portion for Aaron and his sons

"And the holy garments of Aaron shall be for his sons after him, that in them they may be anointed and ordained."
Exodus 29:29 NASB

- Moses shall take the ram of consecration and boil its flesh
- Aaron and his sons shall eat the flesh of the ram of consecration

"And thus you shall do to Aaron and to his sons, according to all that I have commanded you; you shall ordain them through seven days."
Exodus 29:35 NASB

- A bull shall be offered each of the seven days as a sin offering
- Each day you shall cleanse the altar and sanctify it

Altar of Incense

The consecration of Aaron and his sons focused primarily on the altar of burnt sacrifice near the door of the tabernacle.

Apparently neither the altar of incense nor the ingredients of the incense had at that time been revealed to Moses.

"Moreover, you shall make an altar as a place for burning incense; you shall make it of acacia wood.

Its length shall be a cubit, and its width a cubit, it shall be square, and its height shall be two cubits; its horn shall be of one piece with it.

And you shall overlay it with pure gold, its top and its sides all around, and its horns; and you shall make a gold molding all around for it."
Exodus 30:1-3 NASB

The altar of incense would play a major part on the Day of Atonement.

"And Aaron shall make atonement on its horns once a year; he shall make atonement on it with the blood of the sin offering of atonement once a year throughout your generations. It is most holy to the LORD."
Exodus 30:10 NASB

In addition, incense would be burned daily, perpetually, as well as on the Day of Atonement.

The ingredients of the incense were also explicit as God revealed them to Moses.

"Take for yourself (sweet) spices, stacte and onycha and galbanum, spices with pure frankincense; there shall be an equal part of each."
Exodus 30:34 NASB

'Sweet' means 'sweet aroma' and 'stacte,' 'onycha', and 'galbanum' are all known for their aromatic qualities, while 'frankincense' is known for its pure white smoke.

And then God made it very clear not to deviate from His instructions.

"You shall not offer any strange incense on this altar (altar of incense)...

And the incense which you shall make, you shall not make in the same proportions for yourselves, it shall be holy to you for the LORD.

Whoever shall make any like it, to use as perfume, shall be cut off from his people."
Exodus 30:9a, 37-38 NASB

Aaron's sons, however, for whatever reason, disregarded God's explicit instructions.

Now Nadab and Abihu, the sons of Aaron, took their respective firepans, and after putting fire in them, placed incense on it and offered strange (profane) fire before the LORD, which He had not commanded them.
Leviticus 10:1 NASB

The word 'profane' in Hebrew means 'deviating.' In other words, they used a holy thing for something not permitted.

And fire came out from the presence of the LORD and consumed them, and they died before the LORD.

Then Moses said to Aaron, "It is what the LORD spoke..."
Leviticus 10:2-3a NASB

God spoke to Moses shortly after the death of Aaron's sons.

"By those who come near Me I will be treated as holy, and before all the people I will be honored."
Leviticus 10:3b NASB

God had killed Aaron's sons because they disobeyed His commandments regarding the altar of incense located before the veil of the Most Holy Place.

Israel Broke the Old Covenant

Israel did not abide by the old covenant as confirmed by Jeremiah eight hundred years after the old covenant was ratified; but God's grace would prevail.

"Behold, days are coming," declares the LORD, "when I will make a new covenant with the house of Israel and with the house of Judah..."
Jeremiah 31:31 NASB

The Hebrew word for 'new' in this verse is *chadash* with synonyms including 'repair,' 'renew,' and 'fresh.'

"...not like the covenant which I made with their fathers in the day I took them by the hand to bring them out of the land of Egypt, My covenant which they broke, although I was a husband to them," declares the LORD.
Jeremiah 31:32 NASB

Chapter 4

The New Covenant also Ratified with Blood

The Old Covenant was predestined to fail for the following reasons.

"For whoever keeps the whole law and yet stumbles in one point, he has become guilty of all."
James 2:10 NASB

"...nevertheless knowing that a man is not justified (declared righteous) by the works of the Law...since by the works of the Law shall no flesh be justified."
Galatians 2:16 NASB

Jesus Fulfilled the Law

When Jesus came to earth, His mission was to fulfill the law, which no mortal man could do.

"Do not think that I came to abolish the Law or the Prophets; I did not come to abolish, but to fulfill.

For truly I say to you, until heaven and earth pass away, not the smallest letter or stroke shall pass away from the Law, until all is accomplished."
Matthew 5:17-19 NASB

Thus the God/Man Jesus fulfilled the law in its entirety and went to the cross to pay the penalty for all who could not fulfill the law themselves.

By fulfilling the law, Jesus in essence fulfilled the Old Covenant. The New Covenant is spiritual.

Just before Jesus went to the cross, He instituted the New Covenant to replace the Old.

After celebrating the Passover meal with His disciples, He took the cup and said to them:

"Drink from it, all of you;

...for this is My blood of the (new) covenant, which is shed for many for the remission of sins."
Matthew 26:27-28 NKJV

The Greek word for 'new' in this verse is *kainos* meaning 'qualitatively new,' or 'better' than the old.

The days would come when the Spirit of God would reside within His elect of Israel.

As was the Old Covenant, the New Covenant was ratified unilaterally with blood; this time with the blood of Christ when He gave Himself on the cross.

And then Jesus said that he wouldn't drink of the fruit of the vine again until the day that He would drink it with them in His Father's kingdom.

That would be the millennial kingdom after the tribulation when Jesus will rule the nations from Jerusalem.

The New Covenant Described

Perhaps the best description of the New Covenant as it relates to Israel is found in the prophets.

"Behold, days are coming," declares the LORD, "when I will make a new covenant with the house of Israel and with the house of Judah,

... not like the covenant which I made with their fathers in the day I took them by the hand to bring them out of the land of Egypt, My covenant which they broke, although I was a husband to them," declares the LORD.
Jeremiah 31:31-32 NASB

"But this is the covenant which I will make with the house of Israel after those days," declares the LORD,

"...I will put My law within them, and on their heart I will write it; and I will be their God, and they shall be My people.

...for I will forgive their iniquity, and their sin I will remember no more."
Jeremiah 31:33-34b NASB

God confirms that the covenant He made with Israel, when He delivered them out of Egyptian bondage, was broken by the Israelites, even though they said they would obey all of His commands.

Then God said that He will make a new covenant with Israel, whereby He would put His law in their minds, and write it on their hearts.

Such is the work of the Holy Spirit.

The Prophets Spoke of the Spirit to Come to Israel in the Future

Approximately one hundred years before Jeremiah revealed the New Covenant, Isaiah wrote of the coming Messiah being anointed with the Holy Spirit.

"Then a shoot will spring from the stem of Jesse, and a branch from his roots will bear fruit.

And the Spirit of the LORD will rest on Him, the spirit of wisdom and understanding, the spirit of counsel and strength, the spirit of knowledge and the fear of the LORD." Isaiah 11:1-2 NASB

But then God said that the day would come first when He would prevent the Israelites from understanding their future, for a time.

"For the LORD has poured over you a spirit of deep sleep, He has shut your eyes, the prophets; and He has covered your heads, the seers.

And the entire vision shall be to you like the words of a sealed book, which when they give it to the one who is literate, saying, 'Please read this,' he will say, 'I cannot, for it is sealed.'"
Isaiah 29:10-11 NASB

Subsequently Isaiah spoke of the time when the blinders would be removed from the eyes of Israel.

"And as for Me, this is My covenant with them," says the LORD: "My Spirit which is upon you, and My words which I have put in your mouth, shall not depart from your mouth,

... nor from the mouth of your offspring, nor from the mouth of your offspring's offspring," says the LORD, "from now and forever."
Isaiah 59:21 NASB

Approximately one hundred years before Isaiah prophesied, the prophet Joel also spoke of the time when Israel would see.

"And it will come about after this that I will pour out My Spirit on all mankind; and your sons and daughters will prophesy, your old men will dream dreams, your young men will see visions.

And even on the male and female servants I will pour out My Spirit in those days."
Joel 2:28-29 NASB

And then about the time Jerusalem and Judah were sent captive to Babylon, Ezekiel spoke of Israel's future with the Spirit of God.

"And I shall give them one heart, and shall put a new spirit within them. And I shall take the heart of stone out of their flesh and give them a heart of flesh,

... that they may walk in My statutes and keep My ordinances, and do them. Then they will be My people, and I shall be their God."
Ezekiel 11:19-20 NASB

"And I will put My Spirit within you, and you will come to life, and I will place you on your own land. Then you will know that I, the LORD, have spoken and done it," declares the LORD.
Ezekiel 37:14 NASB

Therefore, the day is coming when Israel will be restored, renewed, and have the Spirit of God within them.

The Holy Spirit, however, is the Heart of the Church Today

As the death of Jesus was approaching, He told His disciples that He would be departing to be with His Father. Their feelings were that of sorrow.

"But I tell you the truth, it is to your advantage that I go away; for if I do not go away, the Helper shall not come to you; but if I go, I will send Him to you."
John 16:7 NASB

And then Jesus tells His disciples that the Holy Spirit will do for them what God promised to Israel, i.e., dwell within them.

"And I will ask the Father, and He will give you another Helper, that He may be with you forever;

...that is the Spirit of truth, whom the world cannot receive, because it does not behold Him or know Him, but you know Him because He abides with you, and will be in you."
John 14:16-17 NASB

Recall, shortly after Jesus' ascension, the Holy Spirit made His appearance in grand form on the Day of Pentecost.

And suddenly there came from heaven a noise like a violent, rushing wind, and it filled the whole house where they were sitting.

And they were all filled with the Holy Spirit...
Acts 2:2, 4a NASB

Recall also when Peter was preaching to the household of Cornelius; as they were intently listening; the Jews were astonished when they witnessed Gentiles also receiving the Holy Spirit.

While Peter was still speaking these words, the Holy Spirit fell upon all those who were listening to the message.

And all the circumcised believers who had come with Peter were amazed, because the gift of the Holy Spirit had been poured out upon the Gentiles also.
Acts 10:44-45 NASB

The Holy Spirit Described in the Epistles

Later in the epistles, Paul discussed the Holy Spirit with the churches. He tells of the Holy Spirit teaching believers things far above man's wisdom.

"Now we have received, not the spirit of the world, but the Spirit who is from God, that we might know the things freely given to us by God,

...which things we also speak, not in words taught by human wisdom, but in those taught by the Spirit, combining spiritual thoughts with spiritual words.

But the natural man does not accept the things of the Spirit of God; for they are foolishness to him, and he cannot understand them, because they are spiritually appraised."
1 Corinthians 2:12-14 NASB

And then Paul teaches the church at Ephesus the power of the Holy Spirit to guarantee their eternal inheritance upon their confession of Christ.

"In Him, you also, after listening to the message of truth, the gospel of your salvation – having also believed, you were sealed in Him with the Holy Spirit of promise,

...who is given as a pledge (guarantee) of our inheritance, with a view to the redemption of God's own possession, to the praise of His glory."
Ephesians 1:13-14 NASB

National Israel Waits for what the Church already has

Thus, while the Holy Spirit is very active in the Church during the present age; how about the Israelites?

"What then? That which Israel is seeking for, it has not obtained, but those who were chosen obtained it, and the rest were hardened..."
Romans 11:7 NASB

...Just as it is written: "God has given them a spirit of stupor, eyes that they should not see and ears that they should not hear, to this very day."
Romans 11:8 NKJV

While Israel is in 'a spirit of stupor' during the present age, the Church is filled with the Holy Spirit.

Therefore, the New Covenant, as applied to Israel, will be accomplished in the future; inasmuch as they will also be given the Holy Spirit.

As previously mentioned, to have God's laws in their minds and in their hearts is the work of the Holy Spirit.

Christ is the Mediator of the New Covenant

The Mediator of the New Covenant is the same for both the church and Israel.

Let's first review several examples of 'mediator' in the Old Testament.

There are two predominant Hebrew words translated mediator. The first one is *Yakhach* which also means 'arbitrator.'

For example, when Job was pleading his case before God he said that there was not a mediator that could represent both himself and God.

"For He is not a man, as I am, that I may answer Him, and that we should go to court together. Nor is there any mediator between us, who may lay his hand on us both." Job 9:32-33 NKJV

The same Hebrew word is used in a very popular verse in Isaiah when God was inviting Israel to consider their sin condition and His remedy.

"Come now, and let us reason together..."
Isaiah 1:18 NASB

The phrase 'reason together' is also from *Yakhach*.

And then the Hebrew word *Palal* used for mediator has several synonyms including 'entreat,' 'supplication,' 'intercede,' and 'pray.'

"If one man sins against another, God will mediate for him; but if a man sins against the LORD, who can intercede for him?"
1 Samuel 2:25 NASB

As mentioned previously, approximately 500 years earlier, the people had asked Moses to be their mediator between them and God.

Now all the people witnessed the thunderings, the lightning flashes, the sound of the trumpet, and the mountain smoking; and when the people saw it, they trembled and stood afar off...

... Then they said to Moses, "You speak with us, and we will hear; but let not God speak with us, lest we die."
Exodus 20:18-19 NKJV

The following verse reflects Moses' response to the Israelites' request.

"I stood between the LORD and you at that time, to declare to you the word of the LORD; for you were afraid because of the fire, and you did not go up the mountain."
Deuteronomy 5:5 NKJV

Then in the New Testament the Greek word for mediator is *mesites,* meaning 'middle' or 'go-between.'

We find this word in the epistles when Paul spoke of the mediator between Moses and God when the law was given.

"...and it was appointed through angels by the hand of a mediator."
Galatians 3:19 NKJV

And then in Paul's first letter to Timothy, he told of Christ's position as Mediator, for both Israel and the church.

"For there is one God, and one mediator also between God and men, the man Christ Jesus,

...who gave Himself as a ransom for all, the testimony borne at the proper time."
1 Timothy 2:5 NASB

The Ultimate Mediator is Described in the Book of Hebrews

The writer of the Book of Hebrews told of Christ being the Mediator of the New Covenant.

But now He has obtained a more excellent ministry, inasmuch as He is also Mediator of a better covenant, which was established on better promises.
Hebrews 8:6 NKJV

The 'better covenant' means the New Covenant. God acknowledged limitations in the Old Covenant, inasmuch as it couldn't achieve His ultimate purpose.

For if that first covenant had been faultless, then no place would have been sought for a second. Because finding fault with them He says...

..."Behold, the days are coming," says the LORD, "when I will make a new covenant with the house of Israel and with the house of Judah – not according to the covenant that I made with their fathers..."
Hebrews 8:7-9 NKJV

In that He says, "A new covenant," He has made the first obsolete. Now what is becoming obsolete and growing old is ready to vanish away.
Hebrews 8:13 NKJV

And then, near the end of the Book of Hebrews, the writer wonderfully compares God's presence at Mount Sinai with the future heavenly city, New Jerusalem, where the New Covenant is ultimately fulfilled.

"For you have not come to the mountain that may be touched and that burned with fire, and to blackness and darkness and tempest...

...and the sound of a trumpet and the voice of words, so that those who heard it begged that the word should not be spoken to them anymore."
Hebrews 12:18-19 NKJV

These verses describe the fear of the Israelites when God descended to Mount Sinai in a cloud and spoke to Moses announcing the Ten Commandments. The sights and sounds of God's presence put total fear in the hearts of the Israelites as they considered the likelihood of being killed.

This was the point when the Israelites requested Moses to be the mediator between them and God as previously mentioned.

But then, as a former preacher and friend of mine explained, the very next word in the comparison of Mount Sinai and the heavenly city was a 'cosmic conjunction,' it was the word 'but.'

"But you have come to Mount Zion and to the city of the living God, the heavenly Jerusalem, and to myriads of angels,

...to the general assembly and church of the first-born who are enrolled in heaven, and to God, the judge of all, to the spirits of righteous men made perfect,

... and to Jesus, the mediator of a new covenant, and to the sprinkled blood, which speaks better than the blood of Abel."
Hebrews 12:22-24 NASB

The writer explains that 'the general assembly and church of the firstborn enrolled (registered) in heaven' represents a festive gathering of innumerable angels in New Jerusalem, plus members of the church whose members' names were in the Book of Life, and Jesus is the Head.

The 'spirits of righteous men made perfect' include those of all ages who were perfected (completed the race) because of their faith.

It is confirmed that Jesus is the Mediator of the New Covenant, inasmuch as He shed His blood once for all for the remission of sins. The blood of an animal offered by Abel could only cover his sins for a time, waiting for the blood of the Son of God to pay for those sins in full, forever.

The Testator Must first Die before His Will and Testament is Enacted

"For where there is a testament, there must also of necessity be the death of the testator."
Hebrews 9:16 NKJV

The Greek word for 'testament' in this verse is *diatheke* with several significant synonyms including 'will,' 'unconditional promise,' 'unilateral,' 'divine order,' 'irreversible,' and 'disposition made in prospect of death.'

"For a testament is in force after men are dead, since it has no power at all while the testator lives."
Hebrews 9:17 NKJV

The Greek word for testator is *diatithemai* meaning 'bequeath,' 'purpose,' and 'determine beforehand.'

Thus, Christ's death was necessary in order for God's promise of the New Covenant to be enacted.

"Therefore not even the first covenant was dedicated without blood."
Hebrews 9:18 NKJV

'Blood' was used in this verse replacing 'death' in verses 16 and 17.

The Greek word for 'covenant' in this verse is the same word used for testament, i.e. *diatheke*.

The Old Testament was also ratified with the sprinkling of blood, confirming the death of the animal providing the blood.

Christ is also the Ultimate High Priest

Let's begin by confirming the significance of the fact that Jesus was entirely God, and entirely man. Such was absolutely necessary for Jesus to be the ultimate High Priest.

The writer of the Book of Hebrews reveals much about the deity and humanity of Christ.

"God, who at various times and in various ways spoke in time past to the fathers by the prophets..."
Hebrews 1:1 NKJV

The KJV uses the word 'diverse' instead of various, which is from the Greek words *polus* meaning 'many,' and *tropos* meaning 'manner.' In other words, God communicated to His people in numerous, different ways through the ages to enlighten them to His plan and intention.

"...has in these last days spoken to us by His Son, whom He has appointed heir of all things, through whom also He made the worlds..."
Hebrews 1:2 NKJV

The term 'last days' refers to the time of the Messiah. Another common phrase is 'end of the ages.' This age commonly known as the 'church age' began with the advent of the Messiah and will end with His return.

Being the 'heir of all things' speaks of Christ's deity inasmuch as Christ made the 'worlds.' Everything created was done through Christ's power.

'Worlds' in this context is from the Greek *aionas* meaning periods of time, or ages, but would also include the characteristics of those ages.

"...who being the brightness of His glory and the express image of His person, and upholding all things by the word of His power, when He had by Himself purged our sins, sat down at the right hand of the Majesty on high..."
Hebrews 1:3 NKJV

The word 'brightness' in this context means light being 'emitted' instead of light being 'reflected.' Christ is the source of the light.

Express 'image' means 'corresponding to the original pattern.' The incarnated Christ is the representation of God the Father.

To uphold all things means to be totally in charge.

After Christ had purged our sins, He was resurrected and ascended to sit in the place of power, i.e. at the right hand of God the Father.

The Greek word for 'purge' in the above is *katharismos* which means to remove. It further specifies that such removal could only be done via a mediator.

As the Son of God, Jesus the High Priest is Superior to Angels

"...having become so much better than the angels, as He has by inheritance obtained a more excellent name than they...For to which of the angels did He ever say: 'You are

My Son...I will be to Him a Father...Let all the angels of God worship Him.'"
Hebrews 1:4-6 NKJV

Then the author turns his attention to the humanity of Christ.

"Since then the children share in flesh and blood, He Himself likewise also partook of the same, that through death He might render powerless him who had the power of death, that is, the devil."
Hebrews 2:14 NASB

Just as Jesus was fully God, He was also fully man.

Jesus was born to die so that He could defeat the devil by His resurrection. Also, the wages of sin is death which required Jesus to shed His blood and die in order to pay the sin debt for all mankind.

"Therefore, He had to be made like His brethren in all things, that He might become a merciful and faithful high priest in things pertaining to God, to make propitiation for the sins of the people."
Hebrews 2:17 NASB

'Had to be made' means 'of necessity.'

To be the Mediator of the New Covenant, and the ultimate High Priest, Jesus had to be in the likeness of those for whom He was mediating and serving as High Priest.

To make 'propitiation' for the sins is expressed in the KJV as 'reconciliation.'

The Greek word for reconciliation is *hilaskomai* which means that the High Priest made reconciliation for the sins of the people by sacrificing Himself, revealing His mercy and faithfulness. Christ's merciful act provided the sinner access to God.

Comparing Moses with the Ultimate High Priest

The writer of Hebrews meticulously and objectively exalts Jesus by describing His calling, with other of God's people and their calling.

After comparing Jesus' authority and superiority with angels, the writer of Hebrews provides a comparison of Jesus with Moses.

Everybody under the old covenant knew and loved Moses.

"Therefore, holy brethren, partakers of a heavenly calling, consider Jesus, the Apostle and High Priest of our confession."
Hebrews 3:1 NASB

This is the only time that Jesus is referred to as an Apostle, i.e. one who is sent. In the present context, Jesus serving as an Ambassador of God was sent into the world by His Father to save the world.

The author addresses the holy brethren, partakers of the heavenly calling.

Such defines the members of the household of God who will dwell in the future New Jerusalem.

The brethren are told to consider (learn thoroughly, perceive fully) that Jesus is also called the High Priest 'of our confession' which means that they have a common faith of which they can agree with full assurance and confess boldly and without fear that Jesus was appointed by the Father.

"He was faithful to Him who appointed Him, as Moses also was in all His house."
Hebrews 3:2 NASB

'House' is from the Greek *oikos* meaning family, Jewish assembly, or household of God.

Moses was faithful in his appointment to the Israelites to lead them from bondage in Egypt and to proclaim the law and the Old Covenant.

But Jesus was more faithful than Moses because Jesus built the house (people) that Moses served in as a servant.

"For He has been counted worthy of more glory than Moses, by just so much as the builder of the house has more honor than the house.

For every house is built by someone, but the builder of all things is God."
Hebrews 3:3-4 NASB

Thus while Moses was faithful as a servant in the house to which he was called, he was pointing to future things of which Christ would be the Master of His own house.

"Now Moses was faithful in all His house as a servant, for a testimony of those things which were to be spoken later;

... but Christ was faithful as a Son over His house whose house we are, if we hold fast our confidence and the boast of our hope firm until the end."
Hebrews 3:5-6 NASB

The Work of the High Priest Brings Rest

The doctrine of 'rest' as described in the Epistle to the Hebrews has two connotations. The first 'rest' is defined as the rest for the Israelites from their enemies in the Promised Land if they would be faithful and obedient.

The Hebrew word for this 'rest' is *menuwchah* with multiple meanings including 'ease,' 'comfortable,' 'quiet,' and 'peace.'

Of course that didn't happen, inasmuch as the Israelites rebelled against their leaders and God.

Nearly six hundred years later the Psalmist told of Israel's disobedience in the wilderness and the consequence.

"For forty years I loathed that generation, and said they are a people who err in their heart, and they do not know My ways.

Therefore I swore in My anger, truly they shall not enter into My rest."
Psalms 95:10-11 NASB

Through disobedience and lack of faith, the Israelites broke the Old Covenant, resulting in death to that first generation.

However; the writer of Hebrews states that the promise of rest still remains.

"For if Joshua had given them rest, He would not have spoken of another day after that.

There remains therefore a Sabbath rest for the people of God."
Hebrews 4:8-9 NASB

"Therefore, let us fear lest, while a promise remains of entering His rest, any one of you should seem to have come short (missed the opportunity) of it.

For we who have believed enter that rest, just as He has said..."
Hebrews 4:1, 3 NASB

The 'rest' spoken of in these verses speaks of better things.

"Let us therefore be diligent to enter that rest, lest anyone fall through following the same example of disobedience."
Hebrews 4:11 NASB

The writer of Hebrews exhorted the current generation not to follow the example set by their fathers fourteen hundred years earlier.

He exhorted them to believe and have faith in the word of God.

"Take care, brethren, lest there should be in any one of you an evil, unbelieving heart, in falling away from the living God.

But encourage one another day after day, as long as it is still called 'Today,' lest any one of you be hardened by the deceitfulness of sin."
Hebrews 3:12-13 NASB

The word 'today' in both Hebrew and Greek means 'present,' 'now,' 'this very day.'

The 'rest' available to the Jews during the forty year wilderness journey was just a precursor for eternal rest offered to the current generation.

'Rest' for the current generation meant no more labor (under the law) to achieve righteousness. Faith and obedience were still the keys.

And figuratively, 'rest' also alludes to the future, eternal, abode in heaven.

This final rest is mindful of the 'rest' described in Genesis when God rested from His works of creation.

"And by the seventh day God completed His work... and He rested on the seventh day from all His work which He had done."
Genesis 2:2 NASB

'Rested' in this verse is from the Hebrew *Shavath* meaning to 'cease,' or 'come to an end.'

"For the one who has entered His rest has himself also rested from his works, as God did from His."
Hebrews 4:10 NASB

The writer of Hebrews is explaining to the current generation of Jews not to go back to the law, but cease from such effort to please God. God's eternal rest is available to those with faith in the vicarious death of Jesus.

The 'rest' that is available to all generations is based on God's work from eternity past.

"...although His works were finished from the foundation of the world."
Hebrews 4:3b NASB

That brings to mind a favorite verse from the Book of Acts.

"Known to God from eternity are all His works."
Acts 15:18 NKJV

The sovereignty of God, who devised His plan for mankind from the foundation of the world, is incomprehensible.

And again, the eternal 'rest' is only possible by the works of the great High Priest.

Melchizedek and the Ultimate High Priest

Between the time that Abram was called from across the river Euphrates and the time that God ratified His covenant with him, Abram met Melchizedek.

The setting was when pagan kings Amraphel, Arioch, Chedorlaomer and Tidal attempted to overtake several kingdoms to the south, including Sodom, the home of Abram's nephew Lot.

During the attempted conquest, Lot was taken captive along with his possessions.

As it turned out, there was one who escaped and reported to Abram that his nephew had been taken captive.

When Abram heard the news, he gathered together his trained servants and they pursued after the enemy. He overtook the enemy and recovered his nephew and his goods.

As Abram was returning to his land, the king of Sodom met him.

But before he could talk to Abram, Melchizedek approached Abram.

And Melchizedek king of Salem brought out bread and wine; now he was a priest of God Most High.
Genesis 14:18 NASB

Melchizedek was both king and priest of 'God Most High' and brought gifts and blessings to Abram.

And he (Melchizedek) blessed him (Abram) and said: "Blessed be Abram of God Most High, Possessor of heaven and earth; and blessed be God Most High, who has delivered your enemies into your hand."
Genesis 14:19-20a NASB

And Abram responded:

And he (Abram) gave him (Melchizedek) a tithe of all.
Genesis 14:20b NASB

Melchizedek's name meant 'king of righteousness.' He was, in fact, a man who was serving the 'God Most High' as king and chief priest. He was the king of Salem which meant 'just,' 'quiet,' and 'perfect.' Salem was the early name of Jerusalem.

The 'God Most High' was also the 'Possessor of heaven and earth,' which meant that He owned them. Interestingly, 'possessor' also means 'redeemer.'

And a 'tithe' was a tenth part of the recovered goods.

Abram acknowledged Melchizedek's authority, inasmuch as when he was speaking to the king of Sodom, he referred also to 'God Most High, the Possessor of heaven and earth.'

Approximately a millennium later King David was speaking of the future Messiah's reign and he said:

"The LORD has sworn and will not change His mind, 'Thou art a priest forever according to the order of Melchizedek.'"
Psalms 110:4 NASB

David was revealing that the future Messiah would be a priest forever, as well as being Israel's King, as was Melchizedek.

Now fast forward another thousand years.

The writer of the Epistle to the Hebrews in the first century AD had much to add about Melchizedek being the type of High Priest that Christ would be.

At first the writer sets the stage by affirming the story of Melchizedek during the time of Abram.

"For this Melchizedek, king of Salem, priest of the Most High God, who met Abraham as he was returning from the slaughter of the kings and blessed him,

... to whom also Abraham apportioned a tenth part of all the spoils was...king of righteousness, and then also king of Salem, which is king of peace."
Hebrews 7:1-2 NASB

And then the writer of Hebrews adds several significant details.

"Without father, without mother, without genealogy, having neither beginning of days nor end of life, but made like the Son of God, he abides a priest perpetually."
Hebrews 7:3 NASB

And then the writer explains the limits of the Levitical priesthood in detailed steps.

"Now observe how great this man was to whom Abraham, the patriarch, gave a tenth of the choicest spoils."
Hebrews 7:4 NASB

Then the writer confirms that the sons of Levi received tithes, even though they were mortal men.

"And those indeed of the sons of Levi who receive the priest's office have commandment in the Law to collect a

tenth from the people, that is, from their brethren, although these are descended from Abraham."
Hebrews 7:5 NASB

The writer is making the point that the sons of Levi received tithes from men while they were offspring of Abraham who gave tithes to the greater.

"But the one whose genealogy is not traced from them collected a tenth from Abraham, and blessed the one who had the promises."
Hebrews 7:6 NASB

The priest and king Melchizedek blessed Abraham who had received the immutable promise (covenant) of being the father of many nations and a blessing to all nations.

Then the writer states the obvious.

"But without any dispute the lesser is blessed by the greater."
Hebrews 7:7 NASB

Next the writer explains that in the Levitical priesthood mortal men receive tithes, while Melchizedek received tithes and he had no ending.

"And in this case mortal men receive tithes, but in that case one receives them, of whom it is witnessed that he lives on."
Hebrews 7:8 NASB

Then the writer explains that even though Levi received tithes, he also paid tithes to the greater, inasmuch as Levi was yet to be born of Abraham.

"And, so to speak, through Abraham even Levi, who received tithes, paid tithes, for he was still in the loins of his father when Melchizedek met him."
Hebrews 7:9-10 NASB

Jesus' Qualifications for High Priest

Perhaps the most significant qualification for a priest was that he had to be able to identify with those whom he served.

Another qualification for a High Priest was that he must be appointed by God and be immortal.

Let's examine these qualifications in detail to see that Jesus met those required qualifications.

Firstly, only a man, not a spiritual being, could serve as High Priest.

"For every high priest taken from among men is appointed (ordained) on behalf of men in things pertaining to God, in order to offer both gifts and sacrifices for sins..."
Hebrews 5:1 NASB

This verse confirms the appointment of a man by God to the office of high priest. The primary function of the high priest was to offer gifts and sacrifices to God to pay for man's sins, including the sins of the high priest himself. Gifts and sacrifices are considered to be one and the same.

The high priest must be a man in order to identify with the weaknesses of mankind.

"He can have compassion on those who are ignorant and going astray, since he himself is also subject to weakness." Hebrews 5:2 NKJV

Jesus in His humanity was subject to the same challenges and temptations that face all mankind.

The word 'compassion' for other men is from the Greek *metriopatheo* meaning 'to treat with mildness or meekness.' Synonyms include 'bear with tolerance,' 'to be longsuffering,' and/or 'to suffer with another.'

The high priest would offer sacrifices for sins, not only for others, but also for himself.

"...and because of it he is obligated to offer sacrifices for sins, as for the people, so also for himself." Hebrews 5:3 NASB

The office of high priest cannot be of one's own choice; he must be appointed by God.

"And no one takes the honor to himself, but receives it when he is called by God, even as Aaron was." Hebrews 5:4 NASB

"So also Christ did not glorify Himself to become High Priest, but it was He who said to Him: 'You are My Son, today I have begotten You...You are a priest forever according to the order of Melchizedek.'"
Hebrews 5:5-6 NKJV

The writer of Hebrews then describes the suffering that Christ incurred as He was nearing His hour. Jesus knew He would suffer tremendously as He prepared to pay the sin debt for His brethren.

"In the days of His flesh, when He offered up both prayers and supplications with loud crying and tears to Him who was able to save Him from death, and who was heard because of His piety..."
Hebrews 5:7 NASB

The above verse describes Jesus' cries at Gethsemane to His Father, pleading that if there was some other way... But His will was to do the will of His Father.

Jesus dreaded the truth that His Father's wrath on sin required separation, for a moment.

"And about the ninth hour Jesus cried out with a loud voice, saying, 'Eli, Eli, lama sabachthani?' that is 'My God, My God, why have You forsaken Me?'"
Matthew 27:46 NKJV

And even though Jesus was the Son of God, and without sin, He suffered in the place of sinners. He experienced the price of sin.

"...although He was a Son, He learned obedience from the things which He suffered..."
Hebrews 5:8 NASB

Jesus completed His work He was sent to do. By so doing, He was able to provide eternal salvation for all who would embrace the truth.

"...and having been made perfect, He became to all those who obey Him the source of eternal salvation..."
Hebrews 5:9 NASB

The Greek word for 'perfect" is *teleioo* meaning 'to complete by achieving the attended goal.' The word has a rich meaning as applied to Christ.

Jesus completed, or proved, His qualification as Savior of mankind by enduring the testing of suffering set before Him by His Father.

Other synonyms for the Greek *teleioo* (perfected) include 'accomplish,' 'fulfill,' 'finish,' and 'complete.'

And just before Jesus gave up His Spirit on the cross, He said:

"It is finished!"
John 19:30 NKJV

As the writer of Hebrews was summarizing his thoughts on Jesus' qualifications for high priest, he wrote:

"...being designated by God as a high priest according to the order of Melchizedek."
Hebrews 5:10 NASB

God's Immutable Promise

It is impossible for God to lie, and He can swear by none higher than Himself.

"For when God made the promise to Abraham, since He could swear by no one greater, He swore by Himself,

In the same way, God, desiring even more to show to the heirs of the promise the unchangeableness of His purpose, interposed (confirmed) with an oath."
Hebrews 6:13, 17 NASB

Therefore His 'heirs of the promise' have absolute confidence in His word. This absolute confidence can be expressed in the single word, 'hope.'

The relevant Greek word for 'hope' is *elpis* meaning in this context 'the hope of salvation resulting from justification by faith.'

"This hope we have as an anchor of the soul, a hope both sure and steadfast and one which enters within the veil,

...where Jesus has entered as a forerunner for us, having become a high priest forever according to the order of Melchizedek."
Hebrews 6:19-20 NASB

'Anchor' is the Greek *agkura* meaning 'providing stability by being attached to something.' Metaphorically it means 'hope generated by faith allowing one to stand firm.'

The Levitical Priesthood was only a Foreshadow for Better Things

The writer changes his focus to comparing the Levitical priesthood to Christ as the High Priest.

"Now if perfection was through the Levitical priesthood (for on the basis of it the people received the Law), what further need was there for another priest to arise according to the order of Melchizedek, and not be designated according to the order of Aaron?"
Hebrews 7:11 NASB

The word 'perfection' in this verse is *sozo* which means 'salvation,' 'eternal life,' and 'justification' which ultimately means 'spiritual deliverance.'

The writer is saying that if spiritual deliverance and eternal life were possible under the Levitical priesthood, what need would there be for another priest?

If a priest of the order of Melchizedek arose, then the law must be changed.

"For when the priesthood is changed, of necessity there takes place a change of law also."
Hebrews 7:12 NASB

The law would have had to be changed because Christ was not of the tribe of Levi.

"For the one concerning whom these things are spoken belongs to another tribe, from which no one has officiated at the altar.

For it is evident that our Lord was descended from Judah, a tribe with reference to which Moses spoke nothing concerning priests."
Hebrews 7:13-14 NASB

And then the writer explains that if one came in the likeness of Melchizedek, there would be required other major implications.

"And this is clearer still, if another priest arises according to the likeness of Melchizedek,

...who has become such not on the basis of a law of physical requirement, but according to the power of an indestructible life."
Hebrews 7:15-16 NASB

Thus, the fact that Christ was from the tribe of Judah instead of the priestly tribe of Levi is rather small compared to one coming with immortality instead of the mortal.

The writer reminds his readers of Christ's immortality.

"For He testifies: 'You are a priest forever according to the order of Melchizedek.'"
Hebrews 7:17 NKJV

Then, confirmation is presented that explains that the old priesthood could not provide perfection, while the new could.

"For, on the one hand, there is a setting aside of a former commandment because of its weakness and useslessness...

... (for the Law made nothing perfect), and on the other hand there is a bringing in of a better hope, through which we draw near to God."
Hebrews 7:18-19 NASB

Recall, the Greek for 'hope' is *Elpis* meaning 'earnest expectation,' and 'intense anticipation.'

And then the writer provided details on the advantages of a change in the priesthood.

"And inasmuch as He was not made priest without an oath (for they have become priests without an oath, but He with an oath by Him who said to Him,

...'The LORD has sworn and will not relent' "You are a priest forever according to the order of Melchizedek""")...
Hebrews 7:20-21 NKJV

The word 'oath' is the word *shave* meaning 'sworn.' They are synonyms.

Thus, God the Father has sworn to His Son that He is a priest forever and He would never change His mind.

"...by so much more Jesus has become a surety (guarantee) of a better covenant."
Hebrews 7:22 NKJV

'Surety' is from the Greek *egguos* meaning 'confirmation,' 'assurance,' 'evidence,' and 'proof.'
The writer then states that there were many more priests in years past because they were all mortal and passed away.

"And the former priests, on the one hand, existed in greater numbers, because they were prevented by death from continuing,

...but He, on the other hand, because He abides forever, holds His priesthood permanently."
Hebrews 7:23-24 NASB

The differences between the Old Covenant priesthood and the priesthood of Christ are staggering.

One Priest forever!

"Therefore He is also able to save to the uttermost those who come to God through Him, since He always lives to make intercession for them."
Hebrews 7:25 NKJV

The word uttermost is from the Greek *panteles* which means 'always,' 'forever,' and 'eternal.'

Then the writer begins to summarize his argument relating to the superiority of the priesthood of Christ.

"For such a High Priest was fitting for us, who is holy, harmless, undefiled, separate from sinners, and has become higher than the heavens...

...who does not need daily, as those high priests, to offer up sacrifices, first for His own sins and then for the people's...

...for this He did once for all when He offered up Himself."
Hebrews 7:26-27 NKJV

The above is very straight forward. The phrase 'has become higher than the heavens' can be equated with a previous verse.

"Seeing then that we have a great High Priest who has passed through the heavens, Jesus the Son of God..."
Hebrews 4:14 NKJV

The word 'harmless' means 'void of evil,' 'without guile,' and 'innocent.'

"For the Law appoints men as high priests who are weak, but the word of the oath, which came after the Law, appoints a Son, made perfect forever."
Hebrews 7:28 NASB

In all cases, the law was a precursor for the mercy and grace to be given through Christ, the eternal High Priest, and His eternal glory beginning with the New Covenant.

Only Jesus could fulfill the requirements of an eternal High Priest.

As the Original Tabernacle was Patterned after the Heavenly, so was the Priesthood which served in the Earthly Tabernacle

The writer continues the comparison of the great High Priest with Aaron.

As recently stated, we know that we have a high priest, Jesus, who has passed through the heavens, thus:

"...let us hold fast our confession."
Hebrews 4:14b NASB

The Greek word for 'confession' in the present context is *homologia* meaning 'profession' and 'faith.'

"For by one offering He has perfected for all time those who are sanctified."
Hebrews 10:14 NASB

"For we do not have a high priest who cannot sympathize with our weaknesses, but one who has been tempted in all things as we are, yet without sin."
Hebrews 4:15 NASB

As mentioned previously:

"Therefore, He had to be made like His brethren in all things, that He might become a merciful and faithful high priest in things pertaining to God, to make propitiation for the sins of the people."
Hebrews 2:17 NASB

The Levitical High Priest passed through the court of the tabernacle, and the holy place, to enter the Most Holy Place with the blood of animals to offer atonement for his sins and the sins of the people.

"For there was a tabernacle prepared, the outer one, in which were the lampstand and the table and the sacred bread; this is called the holy place.

And behind the second veil, there was a tabernacle which is called the Holy of Holies."
Hebrews 9:2-3 NASB

"Now when these things have been thus prepared, the priests are continually entering the outer tabernacle, performing the divine worship,

... but into the second only the high priest enters, once a year, not without taking blood, which he offers for himself and for the sins of the people committed in ignorance."
Hebrews 9:6-7 NASB

Then the writer confirms that the way to the Holiest of Holies in the heavens was not yet revealed, but was rather symbolic of that which would be revealed in God's timing.

Jesus passed through the heavens to the throne of God to offer His own blood for the remission of sins one time and then sat at the right hand of God.

Recall, as it was explained earlier, the sin offering on the annual Day of Atonement included the following:

"Then Aaron shall offer the bull for the sin offering which is for himself, that he may make atonement for himself and for his household.

Moreover, he shall take some of the blood of the bull and sprinkle it with his finger on the mercy seat on the east side; also in front of the mercy seat he shall sprinkle some of the blood with his finger seven times."
Leviticus 16:6, 14 NASB

Likewise, Aaron would kill a goat and offer its blood for atonement.

"Then he shall slaughter the goat of the sin offering which is for the people, and bring its blood inside the veil, and do with its blood a he did with the blood of the bull, and sprinkle it on the mercy seat and in front of the mercy seat."
Leviticus 16:15 NASB

"And he shall make atonement for the holy place, because of the impurities of the sons of Israel, and because of their transgressions, in regard to all their sins; and thus he shall do for the tent of meeting which abides with them in the midst of their impurities."
Leviticus 16:16 NASB

All of this was done each year on the 10th day of the 7th month.

But Jesus did it one time for remission of all sins of the sanctified forever.

"He made Him who knew no sin to be sin on our behalf, that we might become the righteousness of God in Him."
2 Corinthians 5:21 NASB

"And behold, the veil of the temple was torn in two from top to bottom, and the earth shook; and the rocks were split..."
Matthew 27:51 NASB

The veil separated the holy place from the Most Holy Place. The Most Holy Place represented the presence of God and was only accessible to the high priest once a year on the Day of Atonement.

Thus, redeemed man now had direct access to God, while Jesus sits on God's right hand interceding for the sanctified until the end of the ages.

The writer summarizes his argument later. This time he compared the daily sacrifices required by the Israelites with the one-time offering of Christ of Himself.

"And every priest stands ministering daily ministering and offering time after time the same sacrifices, which can never take away sins;

...but He, having offered one sacrifice for sins for all time, sat down at the right hand of God..."
Hebrews 10:11-12 NASB

David had a vision of these truths one thousand years before Christ was born.

"The LORD says to my Lord: 'Sit at My right hand, until I make Thine enemies a footstool for Thy feet.'"
Psalm 110:1 NASB

High Priestly Duties, the Old vs. the New

"Now the main point in what has been said is this: 'we have such a high priest, who has taken His seat at the right hand of the throne of the Majesty in the heavens,

... a minister in the sanctuary, and in the true tabernacle, which the Lord pitched, not man.'"
Hebrews 8:1-2 NASB

Then the priestly services are compared, i.e. the old vs. the new.

"But when Christ appeared as a high priest of the good things to come, He entered through the greater and more perfect tabernacle, not made with hands, that is to say, not of this creation;

...and not through the blood of goats and calves, but through His own blood, He entered the holy place once for all, having obtained eternal redemption."
Hebrews 9:11-12 NASB

Blood was the required payment for sins; however, the blood of animals could not pay for sins. It had to be the blood of the one who sinned, or that of an innocent, offering His blood for the sins of others.

The truth is reiterated that Christ is the High Priest of the heavenly tabernacle, paid the price for all sin through

His death, and was then resurrected to sit at the right hand of His Father awaiting the end of the age.

If Christ was on earth, He could not have served as High Priest because, as previously stated, He was not of the priestly tribe of Levi. The priests that served under the law were those…

"…who serve a copy and shadow of the heavenly things, just as Moses was warned by God when he was about to erect the tabernacle…"
Hebrews 8:5a NASB

It was then stated that the pattern of the heavenly was to serve for just a season.

The things built with hands, though patterned after the heavenly, could not do what the heavenly High Priest and heavenly tabernacle could do.

"For Christ did not enter a holy place made with hands, a mere copy of the true one, but into heaven itself, now to appear in the presence of God for us;

… nor was it that He should offer Himself often, as the high priest enters the holy place year by year with blood not his own.

Otherwise, He would have needed to suffer often since the foundation of the world; but now once at the

consummation He has been manifested to put away sin by the sacrifice of Himself."
Hebrews 9:24-26 NASB

Several significant high points include:

- Christ did not enter the earthly tabernacle; He was not a lawful earthly High Priest
- Likewise, only Christ entered the heavenly, true tabernacle
- Christ could identify with men; He was made like His brethren
- Christ did not offer the blood of another, He offered His own innocent blood
- Inasmuch as He was sinless, He could impute His righteousness to others
- This single, one time offering, was sufficient to put away sin forever
- Christ will intercede for the sanctified as long as sin remains
- The earthly sacrifice could only cover sin temporarily until the ultimate High Priest offered Himself, paying for sin once for all

"For the Law, since it was only a shadow of the good things to come and not the very form of things, can never by the same sacrifices year by year, which they offer continually, make perfect those who draw near.

But in those sacrifices there is a reminder of sins year by year."
Hebrews 10:1, 3 NASB

And then follows the great basic truth about blood sacrifices.

"For it is impossible for the blood of bulls and goats to take away sins."
Hebrews 10:4 NASB

Recall when Adam and Eve were sent out of the Garden for their sin?

"And the LORD God made garments of skin for Adam and his wife, and clothed them."
Genesis 3:21 NASB

The loss of life of the animal that provided the skins for covering them was the original precursor for blood sacrifices to follow.

The Unforgivable Sin

The unforgivable sin is rejecting the truth of the death and shed blood of Jesus as the remedy for the cleansing of sin.

The writer of Hebrews reminds his readers of the penalty of death for those who rejected Moses' law.

"Anyone who has set aside the Law of Moses dies without mercy on the testimony of two or three witnesses.

How much severer punishment do you think he will deserve who has trampled under foot the Son of God, and has regarded as unclean the blood of the covenant by which he was sanctified, and has insulted the Spirit of grace?"
Hebrews 10:28-29 NASB

Chapter 5

Water Turns to Blood, and
Blood is One with Wine

It was about to be an exciting time for the Israelites. Their four hundred and thirty years of bondage in Egypt was about to come to an end.

They had grown into a great nation and Pharaoh was not about to let them go. They were his slaves.

God had called Moses and his brother Aaron to Himself and told them what they were going to do. We know the story; Moses pleaded with God to have someone else be the spokesman. God consented and told Moses that his brother Aaron could speak on his behalf.

God also told Moses and Aaron that Pharaoh would not release the Israelites. God said that He would harden Pharaoh's heart relative to releasing them. The Bible also said that Pharaoh hardened his own heart.

There were several Hebrew words used for 'harden' including 'strengthen,' 'cruel,' and 'grievous.'

God put His plan in Pharaoh's heart so that it became his thinking.

Therefore, he would have to suffer the consequences for his disobedience.

"...for it is God who is at work in you, both to will and to work for His good pleasure."
Philippians 2:13 NASB

Water Turns to Blood

Then God told Moses the consequences to Pharaoh of not releasing His people.

Thus says the LORD, "By this you shall know that I am the LORD: behold, I will strike the water that is in the Nile with the staff that is in my hand, and it shall be turned to blood."

Then the LORD said to Moses, "Say to Aaron, take your staff and stretch out your hand over the waters of Egypt... that they may become blood..."

So Moses and Aaron did even as the LORD had commanded...and all the water that was in the Nile was turned to blood.
Exodus 7:17, 19-20a NASB

The Hebrew word for 'blood' in the above three verses is *dam*, which is literal blood; predominately referring to blood that has been shed. It is also the Hebrew word expressing the 'juice of grapes' when used metaphorically for blood.

And the fish that were in the Nile died, and the Nile became foul, so that the Egyptians could not drink water

from the Nile. And the blood was through all the land of Egypt.
Exodus 7:21 NASB

Turning the waters in Egypt to blood was just a precursor for what would happen in the near future for the present generation. The Egyptian miracle happened 3,500 years ago, but it should be a vivid reminder of God's power, so the skeptic best take prophecy seriously.

The tenth and final plague for Egypt would be the death of the firstborn from each family. This would initiate the Passover.

In the final book in the Bible, it is announced that the miracle of water turning to blood will be experienced once again during the tribulation; however, this time the effects will be much broader in scope and will affect many more people.

After the seven seals were opened by the Lamb of God, the seven angels who stand before God were given seven trumpets announcing seven more plagues which would be more catastrophic than the seven seals.

The first trumpet doesn't announce water turning to blood, but rather blood was included in hail and fire that was thrown to the earth.

"And the first (angel) sounded, and there came hail and fire, mixed with blood, and they were thrown to the earth;

and a third of the earth was burnt up, and a third of the trees were burnt up, and all the green grass was burnt up."
Revelation 8:7 NASB

Note that it doesn't say 'like blood' but rather the hail and fire were mixed 'with blood.'

Blood in the above verse is from the Greek *haima* defined as the very basis of life.

"And the second angel sounded, and something like a great mountain burning with fire was thrown into the sea; and a third of the sea became blood; and a third of the creatures, which were in the sea and had life, died; and a third of the ships were destroyed."
Revelation 8:8 NASB

There was something 'like a great mountain,' but a third of the sea 'became blood.'

The Greek word for 'became' is *ginomai* meaning to 'come into existence' or simply 'to be.'

A popular usage of the word is illustrated when the devil was tempting Jesus by challenging Him to command 'that these stones become bread.'

Shortly after the second angel sounded his trumpet, John saw another mighty angel who revealed the power of his two witnesses.

"These have the power to shut up the sky, in order that rain may not fall during the days of their prophesying; and they have power over the waters to turn them into blood, and to smite the earth with every plague, as often as they desire."
Revelation 11:6 NASB

Blood at the Height of God's Wrath

After the Lamb opened the seven seals, and the seven angels who stood before God sounded the seven trumpets, an interval was revealed before the seven angels who had the seven last plagues were summoned.

"...for in them the wrath of God is complete."
Revelation 15:1b NKJV

The seven final plagues were described as golden bowls.

"And one of the four living creatures gave to the seven angels seven golden bowls full of the wrath of God, who lives forever and ever."
Revelation 15:7 NASB

The first bowl poured out caused foul and loathsome sores on those who had the mark of the beast. The sores were the same as those that plagued Egypt.

"And the second angel poured out his bowl into the sea, and it became blood like that of a dead man; and every living thing in the sea died."
Revelation 16:3 NASB

The water in the sea became blood.

"And the third angel poured out his bowl into the rivers and the springs of waters; and they became blood."
Revelation 16:4 NASB

After the sea became blood, the rivers and springs became blood.

Notice again in the above scripture passages that the waters didn't turn into something like blood, but the waters either turned into blood, or became blood.

Blood is the Required Payment for Sin

Inasmuch as the life of the flesh is the blood, and the wages of sin is death, then death for the sake of God's justice and wrath is evidenced by the shedding of blood.

"For the wages of sin is death..."
Romans 6:23 NASB

The Greek word for 'death' in this verse is *thanatos* meaning 'as punishment,' 'worthy of death,' or 'rejection from the kingdom of God.'

Other synonyms include 'murder,' and 'slaughter.'

Let's go back and see what the prophets had to say about the shedding of blood to satisfy God's justice and wrath.

"Draw near, O nations, to hear; and listen, O peoples! Let the earth and all it contains hear, and the world and all that springs from it.

For the LORD's indignation is against all the nations, and His wrath against all their armies...He has given them over to slaughter."
Isaiah 34:1-2 NASB

This is a universal warning to all nations. The Hebrew word for 'indignation' is *Qetseph* meaning 'an outburst of anger,' Another major synonym is 'wrath.'

"The sword of the LORD is filled with blood...for the LORD has a day of vengeance, a year of recompense for the cause of Zion."
Isaiah 34:6a, 8 NASB

Vengeance means 'revenge,' 'retaliation,' and 'punishment.' Recompense means 'retribution.'

"And I will feed your (Israel's) oppressors with their own flesh, and they will become drunk with their own blood as with sweet wine."
Isaiah 49:26a NASB

God will mightily shed the blood of Israel's enemies.

The prophet Ezekiel also speaks of shedding the blood of Israel for their sins. God uses the example of Israel committing harlotry with her lovers.

"Therefore, O harlot, hear the word of the LORD."
Ezekiel 16:35 NASB

'Harlot' in this context condemns Israel for illegal contact with other nations and their gods. He further condemns them for offering their children to foreign Gods.

"Moreover, you took your sons and daughters whom you had borne to Me, and you sacrificed them to idols to be devoured."
Ezekiel 16:20 NASB

The shedding of their children's blood would require the shedding of blood of those who offered their children to foreign gods.

"And I will judge you as women who break wedlock or shed blood are judged; I will bring blood upon you in fury and jealousy."
Ezekiel 16:38 NKJV

Synonyms for fury include 'anger,' 'indignation,' and 'wrath' while jealousy means 'ardent zeal' for justice.

God is holy, righteous, and just; therefore, He must take vengeance on those who break His laws and commands, while rejecting His offer of mercy through His Son. Death is due for those who sin against Him without repentance.

Blood and Wine

The discussion of blood and wine will begin in the first book of the Bible and end with the last book of the Bible.

Recall the prophecy of Jacob shortly before he died in Egypt.

Then Jacob summoned his sons and said, "Assemble yourselves that I may tell you what shall befall you in the days to come (last days)."
Genesis 49:1 NASB

The son of interest in Jacob's prophecy is Judah, because not only would Judah be the ancestor of the Messiah, but Judah is also the only one where 'blood' is included in his father's prophecy.

After Jacob reveals that the future King would be of his lineage, he further foretells of Judah's descendant tying his donkey, and his donkey's colt to the choice vine, i.e. the nation of Israel.

And then Jacob reveals a very interesting future for Judah regarding blood.

"He (Judah) washes his garments in wine, and his robes in the blood of grapes."
Genesis 49:11b NASB

Blood in this verse is the Hebrew *Dam*, which in this context means 'juice of grapes' as mentioned earlier.

Now let's fast forward to Isaiah's prophecy which describes several details relative to the future Messiah of the tribe of Judah.

"I have trodden the wine trough alone, and from the peoples there was no man with Me.

I also trod them in My anger, and trampled them in My wrath;

And their life blood is sprinkled on My garments, and I stained all My raiment.

For the day of vengeance was in My heart..."
Isaiah 63:3-4a NASB

Blood in this passage is in reference to actual blood on the Victor's clothes; however, it is from a different Hebrew word, i.e. *Netsach*, which in the present context means 'brilliant juice of grapes.'

The word 'winepress' is also widely used to describe the trampling of grapes to obtain their juice. Winepress is used metaphorically to describe forcing blood from victims just as juice is forced from grapes.

The following imagery describes Messiah's victory march to avenge His people.

"Who is this who comes from Edom, with garments of glowing colors from Bozrah?

Why is Your apparel red, and Your garments like the one who treads in the wine press?"
Isaiah 63:1-2 NASB

We'll see shortly that the above aptly describes the return of the Lion of the tribe of Judah to end the tribulation.

Jeremiah subsequently wrote of God's punishment of His own people by Nebuchadnezzar.

"The Lord has trampled underfoot all my mighty men in my midst; He has called an assembly against me to crush my young men; the Lord trampled as in a winepress the virgin daughter of Judah."
Lamentations 1:15NKJV

The prophet Joel gave warning that God would judge the nations at the end of the age.

"Proclaim this among the nations: 'Prepare for war!'"
Joel 3:9a NKJV

"Let the nations be aroused and come up to the valley of Jehoshaphat, for there I will sit to judge all the surrounding nations.

Put in the sickle, for the harvest is ripe, come, tread, for the wine press is full; the vats overflow, for their wickedness is great."
Joel 3:12-13 NASB

The winepress is full to the extent that the vats overflow. The meaning is that man's wickedness has reached its limit. The harvest is ready, and judgment is nigh.

The word Jehoshaphat means 'Yahweh judges.'

The apostle John confirmed Joel's prophecy, along with that of other prophets, in the final book in the Bible.

"And the angel swung his sickle to the earth, and gathered the clusters from the vine of the earth, and threw them into the great wine press of the wrath of God.

And the wine press was trodden outside the city, and blood came out from the wine press, up to the horses' bridles, for a distance of two hundred miles."
Revelation 14:19-20 NASB

It is widely believed that the battle of Armageddon will take place at the Valley of Jehoshaphat.

Recall Jacob's prophecy to his son Judah.

"He (Judah) washes his garments in wine, and his robes in the blood of grapes."
Genesis 49:11b NASB

The fulfillment of that prophecy will become reality with the return of Christ.

"And I saw heaven opened; and behold, a white horse, and He who sat upon it is called Faithful and True

And He is clothed with a robe dipped in blood; and His name is called The Word of God

And He treads the wine press of the fierce wrath of God, the Almighty."
Revelation 19:11a, 13a, 15b NASB

**Mine eyes have seen the glory of
the coming of the LORD -
He is trampling out the vintage where
the grapes of wrath are stored.
Glory, glory hallelujah!**

Chapter 6

The Shedding of Innocent
Blood Requires Death

As mentioned earlier it was/is a capital offense for a man to spill the blood of an innocent human, inasmuch as man was created in the very image of God.

Israel, however, shed much blood during their history. This sin was as abominable as their idolatry in God's eyes.

The Killing of Infants

The shedding of innocent blood by Israel included the killing of their first born children by offering them to false gods. Such a thing was an abomination to God.

"They even sacrificed their sons and their daughters to the demons, and shed innocent blood, the blood of their sons and their daughters,

...whom they sacrificed to the idols of Canaan; and the land was polluted with the blood."
Psalm 106:37-38 NASB

God said that such an abomination never entered His mind.

"And they built the high places of Baal that are in the valley of Ben-hinnom to cause their sons and their daughters to pass through the fire to Molech,

...which I had not commanded them nor had it entered My mind that they should do this abomination, to cause Judah to sin."
Jeremiah 32:35 NASB

Such departure from the word of God was not only idolatry, but also spiritual adultery, or harlotry.

Some might surmise in today's world that such an abomination compares with the present practice of legalized abortion. Others would argue that a fetus does not become a child until the child is born.

The Bible very clearly addresses the issue. Recall when Isaac's wife Rebekah was with child.

"And Isaac prayed to the LORD on behalf of his wife, because she was barren; and the LORD answered him and Rebekah his wife conceived.

But the children struggled together within her...when her days to be delivered were fulfilled, behold, there were twins in her womb."
Genesis 25:21, 24 NASB

The Hebrew word for 'children' in the above scripture is *Ben* defined as a 'son, child, boy, or young one.' And the

Hebrew base for 'womb' is *Beten* meaning 'belly,' 'within,' or 'inmost part.'

In other words, Rebekah had two living sons within her body. One of those sons was subsequently named Jacob who was later renamed 'Israel.'

The Apostle Paul confirmed the identity and significance of unborn children.

"And not only this, but when Rebecca also had conceived by one man, even by our father Isaac (for the children not yet being born, nor having done any good or evil, that the purpose of God according to election might stand, not of works but of Him who calls)...

...it was said to her, 'The older shall serve the younger.' As it is written, 'Jacob I have loved, but Esau I have hated.'" Romans 9:10-13 NKJV

God had called the brothers by name and had pre-written their part in His master plan devised before the foundation of the world. The Bible succinctly states His calling for the brothers was announced while they were 'not yet being born.'

King David addressed the significance of newly conceived children within their mother's womb as he attempted to express the majesty and sovereignty of God.

"My frame was not hidden from Thee, when I was made in secret...

...Thine eyes have seen my unformed substance; and in Thy book they were all written, the days that were ordained for me, when as yet there was not one of them."
Psalm 139:15-16 NASB

David confirms that God's purpose for His chosen was set in ages past and their days determined, ordained, and planned before they were even formed in their mother's womb. Their days were already numbered and recorded in the Book of Life.

Roe v. Wade has legally allowed the murder of approximately 61 million children.

Such a law brings to mind the words of Jesus to the Pharisees.

And He answered and said to them, "And why do you yourselves transgress the commandment of God for the sake of your tradition?"

"And thus you invalidated the word of God for the sake of your tradition."
Matthew 15:3, 6 NASB

A child is a child whether running across the room into a parent's protective arms or resting in peace within their mother's protective womb awaiting birth.

Shedding Blood of the Innocent is always Condemned

Nearly always when the word 'innocent' in the context of blood shedding is found in the Old Testament, the Hebrew word used is *naqi* which primarily means 'guiltless' or 'blameless.'

While Solomon reined, he wrote many proverbs.

"There are six things which the LORD hates, yes, seven which are an abomination to Him:

...hands that shed innocent blood..."
Proverbs 6:16-17 NASB

About two hundred years after Solomon reined, righteous King Hezekiah ruled over Judah. His son Manasseh; however, didn't follow in his father's foot steps and was a very evil king.

Manasseh undid much of what his father had done by worshipping idols and offering his son in the fire, which was an abomination to the LORD.

"Moreover, Manasseh shed very much innocent blood until he had filled Jerusalem from one end to another...and the LORD would not forgive."
2 Kings 21:16, 24:4 NASB

As God expounded on His case against Israel, bloodshed was one of their abominations, and they felt no guilt of that sin.

"Also on your skirts is found the lifeblood of the innocent poor...yet you said, 'I am innocent...' behold, I will enter into judgment with you because you say, 'I have not sinned.'"
Jeremiah 2:34-35 NASB

God pleads with Israel to amend their ways that they might dwell in their land forever.

"For if you truly amend your ways...if you do not oppress the alien, the orphan, or the widow

...and do not shed innocent blood in this place...then I will let you dwell in this place..."
Jeremiah 7:6-7a NASB

Then God gives Israel reasons for their coming judgment.

"Because they have forsaken Me and...because they have filled this place with the blood of the innocent

...and have built the high places of Baal to burn their sons in the fire as burnt offerings to Baal..."
Jeremiah 19:4-5 NASB

God tells Jeremiah to tell Israel to amend their ways by executing judgment and righteousness.

"Do justice and righteousness...do not shed innocent blood in this place."
Jeremiah 22:3 NASB

God reminds Israel that their fathers were more righteous and just then they are.

"But your eyes and your heart are intent only upon your own dishonest gain, and on shedding innocent blood..."
Jeremiah 22:17 NASB

Bloodshed by Malice

The predominant Hebrew word for bloodshed is *asham* meaning 'guilty,' 'sin,' 'trespass,' or 'offense.'

Another Hebrew word for bloodshed is *shaphakh* meaning 'pour out,' 'anger,' 'slaughter,' or 'murder.'

'Shaphakh' was the word used in God's declaration of capital punishment.

"Whoever sheddeth (shaphakh) man's blood, by man shall his blood be shed (shaphakh;) for in the image of God made he man."
Genesis 9:6 KJV

It is obvious that such bloodshed has a price.

God's proclamation of capital punishment to Noah would be reaffirmed many times.

God explained to Moses that the cities of refuge were provided for anyone who had killed another without malice. However, if one who escaped to such a city was subsequently found guilty, he must pay for his sin with his own blood.

"But if there is a man who hates his neighbor and lies in wait for him and rises up against him and strikes him so that he dies, and he flees to one of these cities...

...then the elders of his city shall send and take him from there and deliver him into the hand of the avenger of blood, that he may die.

You shall not pity him, but you shall purge the blood of the innocent from Israel, that it may go well with you."
Deuteronomy 19:11-13 NASB

Approximately five hundred years later King David pleaded with God to deliver him from the guilt of bloodshed for killing Uriah.

"Deliver me from the guilt of bloodshed, O God, the God of my salvation..."
Psalm 51:12 NKJV

When Saul's son Jonathan was killed by the Philistines, Saul was severely injured by archers. Saul asked his armorbearer to kill him and put him out of his misery. But his armorbearer would not. Then Saul tried to commit suicide by falling on his own sword. He subsequently died.

Thereafter, a young man came from Saul's camp to speak to David. The young man told David that he found Saul leaning on his spear and Saul asked the young man to kill him.

The young man said:

"So I stood beside him and killed him, because I knew that he could not live after he had fallen."
2 Samuel 1:10 NASB

Then David said to him, "How is it you were not afraid to stretch out your hand to destroy the LORD's anointed?" And David called one of the young men and said, "Go, cut him down." So he struck him and he died.

...and David said to him, "Your blood is on your head, for your mouth has testified against you, saying "I have killed the LORD's anointed."
2 Samuel 1:14-16 NASB

'Head' in the phrase 'Your blood is on your head' is from the Hebrew *Rosh,* which in the present context means 'to repay for evil deeds.'

Then during the time of David's son Solomon, we find another example of contending with innocent blood.

David's former military commander, Joab, had defected from David to his son Adonijah, and in the process killed two righteous men.

King Solomon ordered that Joab be killed in retribution.

And the king said to him, "Do as he has spoken and fall upon him and bury him, that you may remove from me and from my father's house the blood which Joab shed without cause.

And the LORD will return his blood on his own head, because he fell upon two men more righteous and better than he and killed them with the sword.

So shall their blood return on the head of Joab and on the head of his descendants forever..."
1 Kings 2:31-33 NASB

Recall, the phrase 'return on the head...' means to recompense for evil deeds.

Israel's Sin of Blood Shedding and the Consequences

As the LORD was describing Israel's sins and His abhorrence towards them, He said:

"So when you spread out our hands in prayer, I will hide My eyes from you, yes, even though you multiply prayers, I will not listen.

Your hands are full of bloodshed."
Isaiah 1:15 NASB

Shortly thereafter, Isaiah reported that those killed innocently will rise up and testify against their murderers.

"For behold, the LORD is about to come out from His place to punish the inhabitants of the earth for their iniquity; and the earth will reveal her bloodshed..."
Isaiah 26:21 NASB

And then Isaiah tells that Israel's sins have separated them from their God.

"But your iniquities have made a separation between you and your God, and your sins have hid His face from you, so that He does not hear.

For your hands are defiled with blood..."
Isaiah 59:2-3a NASB

Israel hadn't changed over the years that followed. Ezekiel records God's condemnation of Israel and her capital city Jerusalem for their bloodshed and idolatry.

And you (Ezekiel) shall say, "Thus says the Lord God, a city shedding blood in her midst...You have become guilty by the blood which you have shed, and defiled by your idols which you have made."
Ezekiel 22:3-4 NASB

Then Ezekiel records God's judgment on Jerusalem. God ordered all the good people to be marked on their foreheads and be spared, but all the others were to be killed by six angels.

Ezekiel inquired of God if He was going to destroy all the remnant of Israel because of the sins of Jerusalem.

Then He said to me, "The iniquity of the house of Israel and Judah is very, very great, and the land is filled with blood, and the city is full of perversion..."

For they say, "The LORD has forsaken the land, and the LORD does not see!"
Ezekiel 9:9 NASB

"And as for Me also, My eye will neither spare, nor will I have pity, but I will recompense their deeds on their own head."
Ezekiel 9:10 NKJV

Duties of the Watchman

Ezekiel was made a watchman for Israel, which carried with it the responsibility of warning the people of God's judgment and wrath, which God had revealed to him.

"When I say to the wicked, 'You shall surely die' and you do not warn him or speak out to warn the wicked from his wicked way that he may live,

... that wicked man shall die in his iniquity, but his blood I will require at your hand."
Ezekiel 3:18 NASB

"Again, when a righteous man turns away from his righteousness and commits iniquity, and I place an obstacle before him,

He shall die, since you have not warned him, he shall die in his sin, and his righteous deeds which he has done shall not be remembered;

...but his blood I will require at your hand."
Ezekiel 3:20 NASB

In other words, Ezekiel would be responsible for another's death because he didn't warn him of the consequences of his sin.

And again:

"Son of man, speak to the children of your people, and say to them: 'When I bring the sword upon a land, and the people of the land take a man from their territory and make him their watchman...

... When he sees the sword coming upon the land, if he blows the trumpet and warns the people, then whoever hears the sound of the trumpet and does not take warning, if the sword comes and takes him away, his blood shall be on his own head...

...But if the watchman sees the sword coming and does not blow the trumpet, and the people are not warned, and

the sword comes and takes any person from among them he is taken away in his iniquity...

...but his blood I will require at the watchman's hand.'"
Ezekiel 33:2-6 NKJV

God then points out some of Israel's sins to Ezekiel, along with their consequences.

"If he lends money on interest and takes increase; will he live? He will not live! He has committed all these abominations, he will surely be put to death; his blood will be on his own head."
Ezekiel 18:13 NASB

The word 'increase' in the above is from the Hebrew *tarbiyth* meaning an unjust gain.

The sacred city of Jerusalem was guilty of blood shed.

"And you, son of man, will you judge, will you judge the bloody city? Then cause her to know all her abominations.

And you shall say, 'thus says the Lord God,' "A city shedding blood in her midst so that her time will come...you have become guilty by the blood which you have shed.""
Ezekiel 22:2-4 NASB

Examples of Bloodshed in the New Testament

During Jesus' time on earth He confronted the Pharisees with their hypocrisy when they told Jesus that if they had lived in the days of their fathers, they would not have been partakers in shedding blood of the prophets.

Jesus soundly denounced them and called them sons of those who murdered the prophets, inasmuch as they wanted to kill Him.

"Therefore, behold, I am sending you prophets and wise men and scribes; some of them you will kill and crucify, and some of them you will scourge in your synagogues, and persecute from city to city,

... that upon you may fall the guilt of all the righteous blood shed on earth, from the blood of righteous Abel to the blood of Zechariah...whom you murdered between the temple and the altar."
Matthew 23:34-35 NASB

Then at the end of the age the apostle John saw that the mother of harlots who reigned over the kings of the earth was also drunk with blood.

"And I saw the woman drunk with the blood of the saints, and with the blood of the witnesses (martyrs) of Jesus."
Revelation 17:6 NASB

The Greek word for 'blood' in this verse is also *haima* which means in this context, 'life taken away by force.'

"And in her was found the blood of prophets and of saints and of all who have been slain on the earth."
Revelation 18:24 NASB

During the great tribulation the Apostle John hears an angel confirm Jesus' justice in His judgments.

"...for they poured out the blood of saints and prophets and Thou hast given them blood to drink. They deserve it."
Revelation 16:6 NASB

When Christ returns to complete the redemption process, He will justifiably shed much blood of His enemies.

The Old Testament reveals innumerable examples of sins that require death. In America some of the same sins that required death in Moses time are protected by law to do such things without penalty today.

Are the watchmen silent?

Chapter 7

The Ultimate Bloodshed –
Behold the Lamb

There were several examples of burnt offerings prior to the Passover which took place the evening before the Israelites left their Egyptian bondage.

Perhaps the most significant pre-Passover example was when Abraham was told to offer his son Isaac as a burnt offering mentioned briefly in an earlier chapter.

The Significance of a Substitute

Both Abraham and Isaac were completely obedient to God's command, and they left to travel to the 'land of Moriah' as instructed.

So Abraham rose early in the morning and saddled his donkey, and took two of his young men with him and Isaac his son; and he split wood for the burnt offering, and arose and went to the place of which God told him.
Genesis 22:3 NASB

Abraham was totally prepared to obey God's command to offer his son.

And Abraham took the wood of the burnt offering and laid it on Isaac his son, and he took in his hand the fire and the knife. So the two of them walked on together.
Genesis 22:6 NASB

But Isaac realized that something was missing.

And Isaac spoke to Abraham his father and said, "My father!" And he said, "Here I am, my son." And he said, "Behold, the fire and the wood, but where is the lamb for the burnt offering?"
Genesis 22:7 NASB

And Abraham said, "God will provide for Himself the lamb for the burnt offering, my son." So the two of them walked on together.
Genesis 22:8 NASB

Abraham placed the wood on the altar, bound his son Isaac, and laid him on the altar. Just as Abraham was about to slay his son, the Angel of the LORD called to him from heaven and told Abraham not to lay his hand on his son.

Then Abraham raised his eyes and looked, and behold, behind him a ram caught in the thicket by his horns, and Abraham went and took the ram, and offered him up for a burnt offering in the place of his son.
Genesis 22:13 NASB

And Abraham called the name of that place The LORD Will Provide, as it is said to this day, "In the mount of the LORD it will be provided."
Genesis 22:14 NASB

Several key points

- Abraham was totally obedient to God's command
- Abraham was willing to offer his son as a sacrifice
- The designated place of the sacrifice would become significant in Israel's future, i.e. the place where Solomon would build the LORD's temple
- Abraham had confidence he would see his son again
- When God saw Abraham's obedience He provided a substitute
- The substitute was a ram, a male of the sheep

Other Events where a Lamb was the Sacrifice, or Substitute

Even before the law was given in the third month after the children of Israel had been delivered from Egyptian bondage, the Passover was initiated.

Details were given in previous chapters; however, we'll summarize several high points here.

- The Israelites were to choose a lamb of the first year without blemish on the tenth day of the first month
- The lamb was to satisfy each man's need

- The lamb was to be killed on the fourteenth day of the first month
- No bone of the lamb was to be broken
- Blood of the lamb was to be sprinkled on the door posts and the lintel of the Israelite's dwelling places
- The lamb was to be eaten on the evening of the fourteenth day with unleavened bread
- During that night the LORD would pass through the land, and the firstborn of both men and beast would be killed, unless the LORD saw the blood of the lamb on the doorposts and lintel
- When the blood was spotted the LORD would pass over that house, sparing the occupants

Subsequent to the Passover, there were many other occasions when lambs were offered as listed below.

- Daily burnt offerings
- Burnt offerings on regular Sabbath days
- Beginning of month burnt offerings
- Spontaneous burnt offerings
- Sin and Trespass offerings
- Feast of Unleavened Bread
- Feast of Weeks
- Feast of Trumpets
- Feast of Tabernacles
- Burnt offerings in the Millennial Kingdom
- The Day of Atonement did not include lambs; however, it did include a ram, just as the substitute

God provided for Abraham when he was willing to offer his son Isaac

The sacrifice of lambs, particularly the Passover Lamb, was a precursor for the ultimate Lamb of God.

When John the Baptist was baptizing, he saw Jesus approaching.

The next day he saw Jesus coming to him, and said, "Behold, the Lamb of God who takes away the sin of the world!"
John 1:29 NASB

While shedding of innocent blood may bring death, the shedding of Christ's innocent blood gives life.

The blood of animals was not sufficient for remission of sins; therefore, the Old Covenant was about to be replaced with the new and ratified with the blood of the Son of God.

The Ultimate Passover Lamb

After Jesus was on earth for approximately three years, the ultimate Passover Lamb was about to be offered for the sins of the world.

Jesus and His disciples observed the Passover feast, or last supper, on the evening before He was crucified. As Jesus took the third Passover cup, He spoke the following to His disciples:

"Drink from it, all of you. For this My blood of the new covenant, which is shed for many for the remission of sins."
Matthew 26:28 NKJV

The Greek word for 'new' is *kainos* meaning something that is better than the old, i.e. qualitatively new.

Paul later confirmed to the church at Corinth the significance of the third cup after the last Passover Supper, and added a requirement.

"In the same way He took the cup also, after supper, saying, 'this cup is the new covenant in My blood; do this, as often as you drink it, in remembrance of me.'"
1 Corinthians 11:25 NASB

Participating in the Lord's Supper and drinking of the cup should bring to remembrance that Jesus, as the Passover Lamb of God, shed His blood for the sins of the world.

Many wonder how Jesus could have eaten the Passover meal with His disciples, yet be crucified on the Passover day.

The Jews from the area around Galilee counted a day from sunrise to sunrise, while the Jews dwelling around Jerusalem counted a day from sunset to sunset.

Therefore, Jesus and His disciples ate the Passover meal on Thursday evening which to them was Passover, and He would be crucified the next day which was Passover to the Jews in Jerusalem.

And this is confirmed by the Jews considering the day in which Jesus was crucified as the day before the Sabbath, or Friday.

And when evening had already come (Friday), because it was the Preparation Day, that is, the day before the Sabbath...
Mark 15:42 NASB

Jesus Was about to Die

Jesus was fully aware of the pre-written history of His three year journey as He prepared for His death. He knew full well that prophecy was about to become reality.

Jesus knew that when He came to earth He would be scorned and held in contempt. He knew that, inasmuch as He came to earth as a normal man without fanfare, that He would not be recognized for who He was.

The leaders of His nation of Israel, even after He gave many signs and wonders, forsook Him and thought He was a blasphemer, inasmuch as He equated Himself with God.

During His time on earth He experienced much grief, which He was prepared for, knowing the thoughts of that generation.

Nevertheless, He knew His purpose was to bear the afflictions of others, while the Jews thought He deserved death for His own sins.

Yes, He knew He would be slaughtered, but not for Himself. Therefore, He would be humbled and crushed for the sins of others.

Jesus would take on Himself the penalty of sin for those who sinned. The result would be that by His vicarious death, the sinful condition of those who killed Him could be made whole.

Those who wanted Him killed were like sheep without a shepherd, inasmuch that there was no leader to protect them, and they would stray away from safety.

God, the Father met with His Son and entreated Him to fulfill His foreordained mission to take on Himself the sins of all mankind.

Jesus, as expected, was distressed and abased; but even considering what was happening to Him, He kept silent, knowing His Father's will would be done.

Jesus would be likened to an innocent Lamb that would not know it was being led to the slaughter; therefore, Jesus did not utter a word in His own defense.

He went willingly to do His Father's will.

Jesus was well aware that seven hundred years before He was born, the prophet Isaiah revealed the travail awaiting Him: His rejection from His own people and His vicarious death on the cross.

"For He grew up before Him like a tender shoot, and like a root out of parched ground; He has no stately form or majesty that we should look upon Him, nor appearance that we should be attracted to Him...

He was despised and forsaken of men, a man of sorrows, and acquainted with grief; and like one from whom men hide their face, He was despised, and we did not esteem Him.

Surely our griefs He Himself bore, and our sorrows He carried; yet we ourselves esteemed Him stricken, smitten of God, and afflicted.

But He was pierced through for our transgressions, He was crushed for our iniquities; the chastening for our well-being fell upon Him, and by His scourging we are healed.

All of us like sheep have gone astray, each of us has turned to his own way; but the LORD has caused the iniquity of us all to fall on Him.

He was oppressed and He was afflicted, yet He did not open His mouth; like a lamb that is led to slaughter and like a sheep that is silent before its shearers, so He did not open His mouth.
Isaiah 53:2-7 NASB

The Trial of Jesus

As Jesus was before the chief priest and elders, and all the council, they brought false witnesses forward.

Recall Jesus response.

And the high priest stood up and said to Him, "Do You make no answer? What is it that these men are testifying against You?" But Jesus kept silent.
Matthew 26:62-63 NASB

The self righteous Jews wanted Jesus killed, but they didn't have the authority to do so; therefore, they delivered Him to Roman authority.

As Jesus stood before Pilate, Pilate offered to release Barabbas to appease the Jews at the Passover. However, the Jews called for Jesus to be killed.

And when Pilate saw that he was accomplishing nothing, but rather that a riot was starting, he took water and washed his hands in front of the multitude, saying, "I am innocent of this Man's blood; see to that yourselves."

And all the people answered and said, "His blood be on us and on our children!"
Matthew 27:24-25 NASB

But it cannot be forgotten that Jesus was the Lamb of God slain from the foundation of the world.

Being the day before the Sabbath caused preordained events to take place.

The Jews therefore, because it was the day of preparation, so that the bodies should not remain on the cross on the

Sabbath (for that Sabbath was a high day), asked Pilate that their legs might be broken, and that they might be taken away.

The soldiers therefore came, and broke the legs of the first man, and of the other man who was crucified with Him; but coming to Jesus, when they saw that He was already dead, they did not break His legs.
John 19:31-33 NASB

One of the soldiers wanted to be sure that Jesus was dead.

But one of the soldiers pierced His side with a spear, and immediately there came out blood and water.
John 19:34 NASB

The blood came first and then the water. Could it be that the water represented the Holy Spirit which was given after the blood was shed?

Apostolic Teaching on the Shed Blood of Christ

The remainder of this chapter will focus on the shed blood of the Passover Lamb; ordained as such from the foundation of the world!

Therefore each of the remaining passages will contain either the word blood, or Lamb.

Recall when Philip was sent by an angel of the Lord to explain Scripture to an Ethiopian who was reading the Book of Isaiah.

The Ethiopian was reading Isaiah 53:6-7 where it describes one being led to the slaughter as a humble, silent lamb.

The Ethiopian asked Philip who the prophet was speaking of, and Philip preached Jesus to him.

Luke later confirmed that the shedding of Christ's blood was the payment for the New Testament church.

"...the Holy Spirit has made you overseers, to shepherd the church of God which He purchased with His own blood." Acts 20:28 NASB

The Greek word for 'purchased' is *peripoieo* meaning to 'gain for oneself,' 'obtain,' and 'acquire.'

'Church' is from the Greek *ekklesia* which represents the New Testament congregation of the redeemed called by, and to, Christ unto salvation.

Paul subsequently confirmed that no one could obey the whole law, and therefore, required a Savior.

"For all have sinned and fall short of the glory of God, being justified as a gift by His grace through the redemption which is in Christ Jesus;

... whom God displayed publicly as a propitiation in His blood through faith. This was to demonstrate His righteousness, because in the forbearance of God He passed over the sins previously committed."
Romans 3:23-25 NASB

There are several key words in this passage.

The Greek word for 'justified' in this passage is from the Greek *dikaioo* meaning to be declared righteous in regard to the law, but not by the law.

The law had to be fulfilled, and it could only be done by Jesus, the Son of God. Justification is a free gift from Almighty God.

The Greek word for 'redemption' in this context is *apolutrosis* meaning deliverance from the power and consequences of sin by paying a ransom. This word is synonymous with purchase *peripoieo* stated above. Another synonym is 'reconcile.'

Propitiation in the above is from the Greek word *hilasterios* meaning Christ was the Lamb slain; as such Christ was the true mercy seat.

Paul confirms that believers have been justified by the blood of Christ, even while we were still in our sinful state.

"But God demonstrates His own love toward us, in that while we were yet sinners, Christ died for us.

Much more then, having now been justified by His blood, we shall be saved from the wrath of God through Him."
Romans 5:8-9 NASB

God's wrath is from the Greek *orge* meaning God's righteous anger and divine judgment reserved for the wicked.

Paul goes on to state that redemption provides forgiveness of sins, and it is solely an act of grace.

"In Him we have redemption through His blood, the forgiveness of our trespasses, according to the riches of His grace."
Ephesians 1:7 NASB

Then Paul reminds us that we were once aliens from God and His people with no hope, but by a proactive act of God we were brought into sonship by the blood of Christ.

"Remember that you were at that time separate from Christ, excluded from the commonwealth of Israel, and strangers to the covenants of promise, having no hope and without God in the world.

But now in Christ Jesus you who formerly were far off have been brought near by the blood of Christ."
Ephesians 2:12-13 NASB

The phrase 'brought near' means to be 'reconciled.'

In his letter to the church at Colosse Paul reiterated that God has brought His elect out of the darkness into the light. And again, it was by redemption by the blood of Jesus.

"He has delivered us from the power of darkness and conveyed us into the kingdom of the Son of His love, in whom we have redemption through His blood, the forgiveness of sins."
Colossians 1:13-14 NKJV

"For it was the Father's good pleasure for all the fullness to dwell in Him, and through Him to reconcile all things to Himself, having made peace through the blood of His cross."
Colossians 2:19-20 NASB

It was God's plan from the foundation of the world to reconcile all things to Himself. The resulting peace was only possible by the shed blood of Christ on the cross.

As the Apostle Peter was addressing the dispersed Christians in other lands, his greeting included the blood of Christ.

"To those who reside as aliens, scattered throughout Pontus, Galatia, Cappadocia, Asia, and Bithynia, who are chosen according to the foreknowledge of God the Father,

...by the sanctifying work of the Spirit, that you may obey Jesus Christ and be sprinkled with His blood: May grace and peace by yours in fullest measure."
1 Peter 1:1-2 NASB

And then Peter explained that redemption was not possible by tangible things of this world that are subject to corruption, even though such things may have great meaning to those of the world.

Peter also confirmed that Christ was foreordained to shed His blood as the Passover Lamb before the foundation of the world.

"Knowing that you were not redeemed with perishable (corruptible) things like silver or gold from your futile way of life inherited from your forefathers,

... but with the precious blood, as of a lamb unblemished and spotless, the blood of Christ.

For He was foreknown before the foundation of the world, but has appeared in these last times for the sake of you..."
1 Peter 1:18-20 NASB

'Corruptible' is from the Greek *phthartos* which means that material things cannot bring spiritual salvation. All material things are subject to decay.

'Redeemed' in these verses is from the Greek *lutroo* meaning 'rescue,' 'deliver,' 'free,' and 'release.' It further signifies that Christ is the redeemer of mankind from bondage.

And lastly John describes God's chosen ones as being delivered from the darkness into the light.

"But if we walk in the light as He Himself is in the light, we have fellowship with one another, and the blood of Jesus His Son cleanses us from all sin."
1 John 1:7 NASB

'Light' in this verse is from the Greek *phos* which means being enlightened by God with true knowledge of spiritual things.

'Fellowship' is from the Greek *koinonia* which means communion and partnership with other believers.

From the Book of Revelation

Then near the end of the first century AD, while the Apostle John was on the Isle of Patmos, he wrote a letter to the seven churches.

In his greeting to the churches, he stated that this letter was from the trinity. He described Jesus thusly:

"To Him who loves us, and released us from our sins by His blood, and He has made us to be a kingdom, priests to

His God and Father; to Him be the glory and the dominion forever and ever."
Revelation 1:5b-6 NASB

Jesus is described as the One who shed His own blood to cleanse us from our sins; He was the sacrifice and the substitute for us.

Shortly thereafter, John heard a voice like a trumpet speaking to him. The voice invited John to heaven to see what was going to happen after the age of the church.

John was immediately in the Spirit in the presence of the throne of Almighty God. Around the throne were twenty-four elders and four living creatures extolling God Almighty.

Then John saw a scroll sealed with seven seals in the hand of Him who sat on the throne.

The seven sealed scroll was the title deed of the earth. But sadly there was found no one worthy to open the scroll and loose its seals.

But one of the elders told John not to weep.

"And I saw between the throne (with the four living creatures) and the elders a Lamb standing, as if slain...

And He came, and He took it (the scroll) out of the right hand of Him who sat on the throne."
Revelation 5:6a, 7 NASB

At that point the four living creatures and the twenty-four elders fell down before the Lamb…

And they sang a new song, saying, "Worthy art Thou to take the book (scroll), and to break its seals; for Thou was slain, and didst purchase for God with Thy blood men from every tribe and tongue and people and nation."
Revelation 5:9 NASB

And then John looked and heard the host around the throne numbering ten thousand times ten thousand, and thousands of thousands…

…saying with a loud voice:

"Worthy is the Lamb who was slain to receive power and riches and wisdom and strength and might and glory and blessing!"
Revelation 5:12 NASB

And then John heard the voices of every living creature in heaven and on earth, under the earth and in the sea saying:

"To Him who sits on the throne, and to the Lamb, be blessing and honor and glory and dominion forever and ever."
Revelation 5:13b NASB

Soon the Lamb is recognized for His power as the tribulation progresses.

Catastrophic geographic events occur and all unrepentant mankind tries to hide themselves from its source.

And the kings of the earth and the great men and the commanders and the rich and the strong and every slave and free man, hid themselves in the caves and among the rocks of the mountains;

...and they said to the mountains and to the rocks, "Fall on us and hide us from the presence of Him who sits on the throne, and from the wrath of the Lamb; for the great day of their wrath has come; and who is able to stand?"
Revelation 6:15-17 NASB

During the reclamation of the earth, war breaks out in heaven between Michael and his angels and the devil and his angels.

At that point the devil and his angels were cast out of heaven to the bottomless pit near the River Euphrates.

Those who were accused and persecuted overcame the war.

And they overcame him because of the blood of the Lamb and because of the word of their testimony, and they did not love their life even to death.
Revelation 12:11 NASB

Then the anti-Christ entered the picture and God gave him the authority and power to make war with the saints and prevail, for three and a half years.

And all who dwell on the earth will worship him, every one whose name has not been written from the foundation of the world in the book of life of the Lamb who has been slain.
Revelation 13:8 NASB

It is interesting to note that the Book of Life belongs to the Lamb, and also that the Lamb of God was foreordained to be slain from the beginning.

And then after the tribulation and the millennial kingdom, when New Jerusalem descends from heaven, the trinity once again is in the presence of mankind.

John is given a vision of New Jerusalem by one of the seven angels.

"Come here, I shall show you the bride, the wife of the Lamb."

And he carried me away in the Spirit to a great and high mountain, and showed me the holy city, Jerusalem, coming down out of heaven from God.
Revelation 21:9b-10 NASB

Christ is the bridegroom of the church, and New Jerusalem will be their home.

And lastly, relative to the Lamb, John is given a vision of the inside of New Jerusalem.

"And he showed me a river of the water of life, clear as crystal, coming from the throne of God and of the Lamb." Revelation 22:1 NASB

The throne of God, i.e. the Father...

The Lamb, i.e. the Son

The river of water of life, i.e. the Holy Spirit

There is nothing new under the sun.

Printed in the United States
By Bookmasters